MY STORY:
Adventures with Holiday On Ice

by
Carl Moseley

Edited by
Julia P. Hardin

Design & Layout by
Fleur-de-lis Designs
Knoxville, Tennessee

My Story: Adventures with Holiday On Ice. Copyright © 2017 by Carl Moseley. All rights reserved. Printed in the United States of America. No part of this book may be used or reproduced in any manner whatsoever without written permission except in the case of brief quotations embodied in articles and reviews discussing this book. For information, contact moseleysk8s@gmail.com.

FIRST EDITION

Moseley, Carl
  My Story: Adventures with Holiday On Ice/Carl Moseley   -- 1st ed.

ISBN 978-0-9991044-1-5
1. Entertainment
2. Performing Arts

Table of Contents

Holiday On Ice U.S.A. 1965: Jacksonville to Mobile

Chapter 1	All Aboard	9
Chapter 2	The Best Ice Show in the World	11
Chapter 3	"Boxoffice"	13
Chapter 4	Learning the Ropes	15
Chapter 5	Taking Care of the Show	17
Chapter 6	From the Ice to the Beach	19
Chapter 7	The In-Between Times	21
Chapter 8	Mr. C & the Record Lady	23
Chapter 9	Show Train & Party Cars	26
Chapter 10	A Few Snags	28
Chapter 11	Deadwood	31
Chapter 12	Rat Holes & Jewel Boxes	34
Chapter 13	The Ins and Outs	36
Chapter 14	A Venerable Venue	38
Chapter 15	Hooray for the Ice Engineers	40

Holiday On Ice U.S.A. 1965: Mexico

Chapter 16	Heading South of the Border	45
Chapter 17	Scotch & A Swim	48
Chapter 18	The Crossing	50
Chapter 19	The Little Engine That Could	52
Chapter 20	Sights and Sounds and Castinets	54
Chapter 21	El Spectacle Holiday	56
Chapter 22	A Bit of Fun Filling In	58
Chapter 23	Horses and Bulls	62
Chapter 24	Tips from the Spin Doctor	65
Chapter 25	One Last Visit to the Chalet Suizo	68

Holiday On Ice U.S.A. 1966: Rehearsals in Knoxville

Chapter 26	A New Beginning	73
Chapter 27	A Perfect Place for Rehearsals	75
Chapter 28	Sloopy, Hang On!	78
Chapter 29	A Special Video Collection	81
Chapter 30	That's the Way You Do It!	84
Chapter 31	Sets & Rigs & the AJ	87
Chapter 32	Mrs. T	90
Chapter 33	The Houn' Dog & A Latin Lover	93
Chapter 34	Levitation & Laughter	96

Table of Contents, Continued

COLOR PHOTO SECTION 99-135

Holiday On Ice U.S.A. 1966: Moving On to the Big Apple

Chapter 35	Memories Are Made of This	139
Chapter 36	A Very Unique Mule Act	141
Chapter 37	The Show Must Go On	144
Chapter 38	Best Laid Plans	146
Chapter 39	Last Show in the Old Garden	148
Chapter 40	The Collins Step	150
Chapter 41	Legends On Ice & On Sawdust	152
Chapter 42	Celebrities & Gypsies	156
Chapter 43	Great Friendships & Food	159
Chapter 44	The Magic Behind the Scenes	162
Chapter 45	Stepping In & Up	164

Holiday On Ice U.S.A. 1965-1968: Some High Points

Chapter 46	It Takes Three, Baby	169
Chapter 47	Skivvies & The Ghost	172
Chapter 48	Comedy & Tragedy	174
Chapter 49	A Really Big Shew	177
Chapter 50	Reno Gals, Oakland Woods	179
Chapter 51	Sonja and Other Stars	182
Chapter 52	Hooray for Hollywood	186
Chapter 53	From the Ice to the Prairie	188
Chapter 54	Landing Your Axel in the Front Row	191
Chapter 55	Elegant Costumes & Fond Memories	194
Chapter 56	Student Successes	196

Before Holiday On Ice 1965-1968: Falling In Love with the Ice

Chapter 57	Barefoot Boy from the South	201
Chapter 58	A Trip Up the McKay Creek	204
Chapter 59	Preserving History	206
Chapter 60	First Pair of Ice Skates	208
Chapter 61	Barrels & Stilts & Penguins	211
Chapter 62	Looking Back	217
Chapter 63	Corralling the Jr Club Kids	220
Chapter 64	Inspiration in Philly	223
Chapter 65	A Tale of Rome	227
Chapter 66	Escape & Evasion	231

About the Author 235

Holiday On Ice 1965 U.S.A.

Jacksonville to Mobile

Chapter One

All Aboard

We arrived, with our luggage, at the train station, right at 10:00 p.m., as that's when Tommy Collins had said the show train could be boarded. My wife, then, Linda, and I were joining *Holiday On Ice*, mid-Spring tour, in Jacksonville, Florida -- she as a skater, replacing Rosita Percelly in the chorus, and me replacing Bob Gaylor, company treasurer, but as Tommy Collins' assistant company manager, as well. The private show train was to leave at 1:00 a.m. from St. Petersburg, but Tommy said, as he was putting us on the train list, that we could get on any time after 10:00 p.m., when the cars would be ready!

Of course, no one else was there, beside the empty private Pullman cars. They were all out partying, or whatever, enjoying their Sunday night off!

Alone, and strange does not adequately describe how we felt, standing there. After a bit, one lonely sole arrived, who we found out later did not take part in any partying (as she had a hubby-to-be in Mexico City). Pretty Adri Verzaal, from Holland, had a berth in what came to be called the "quiet-car," in which car we were also given a bedroom, as were other married couples in the show. Adri was very friendly, understanding, and said much to put us at ease, but she was off to bed soon, and there we were, alone, again.

Not for long, though, as folks like Alice Quessy LeMac and son Ronny arrived soon, after a nice dinner or such, and began filling the Pullman car. Alice's hubby, Joe LeMac, stage manager, wouldn't be along until just before the train pulled out, at 1:00 a.m., as he was supervising the "move-out" at the "building," Bayfront Center Arena. Their bedroom was next to ours on the train that night, and remained so, for the rest of the tour, and the next two tours, as well!

Alice and Joe became good friends, as they, too, lived in Florida (in Clearwater,) and Alice had me coach Ronny through his first figure test the next summer at our rink in St. Petersburg.

But I'm getting away from my story of that first trip...

Holiday On Ice rail "baggage" cars being converted from dining cars in Venice, Florida by Gene Verchesky

Chapter Two

The Best Ice Show in the World

Day one with *Holiday On Ice* in Jacksonville proved rather uneventful, as it was a "travel day," and the show was not set up at the Coliseum until the next day -- opening day. We made new friends that day, however, including Terry Cramer Kessler King, who invited us to share her cab from the train station. Terry skated in the show, and her hubby, Mike Kessler, also a skater, was lighting director that year instead of skating in the show, but Mike and Terry were also aspiring adagio skaters at the time!

About 20 "kids" from the show shared rooms at the small mom and pop motel near the Jacksonville Coliseum, and a pool party was in progress that evening for Rosita Percelly, who was leaving, soon. We were invited, and met many new friends! Fun by all, including dumping of some into the pool with many laughs!

Day two began with my reporting to the building, as the "move-in" was underway! Not yet familiar with the IATSE (the International Alliance of Theatrical Stage Employees), I assumed that the trim fellow who was up and down an extension ladder, adjusting (focusing) stationary down spots on the overhead beams, Jerry Nashleanas, was a skater, doing another job! Just an indication, of all I had yet to learn.

"My Story" by Carl Moseley

I had followed *Holiday On Ice* ever since my dad promoted the show and Ice Vogues, back in 1947 and 48, and I thought I knew a lot about it -- ha! I sure had a lot more to learn. As I'm certain the figure skating director, Nate Walley, thought when we met while watching the move-in that morning. I told Nate that I wanted to see *Holiday On Ice* become the best ice show in the world. Nate looked right at me, and said: "I have news for you - *Holiday On Ice* IS the best ice show in the world!"

We became friends, however, although I think Nate always thought me somewhat assuming. We got into an argument once about Petra Burka's technique in her trademark one-arm overhead double lutz, and I learned a lot from Nate Walley over the next couple of years. Stage Manager Joe LeMac saved the day for me when he welcomed me warmly, and sat down with me to chat, as we watched things progress with the "move-in."

Yes, we opened on time!

Movin' In

Chapter Three

"Boxoffice"

Well, we opened in Jacksonville that first week, and I began to get a handle on what my new job was all about! One other lasting impression during the move-in opening day was this gal in Bermuda shorts bringing in a sandwich or lunch bag for, as I found out later, her electrician boyfriend. "Gooch," as was her nickname, turned out to be Lucille (Lucy) Carpenter, line captain, who also became a long-time good friend.

Joe LeMac, stage manager (a rock, on whom I relied on many a time over the next few years) showed me to the room in the Jacksonville Coliseum to which we had been assigned for our *Holiday On Ice* office, as the HOI blue office file crates on casters (as were all HOI crates) had arrived there. Every crate was on wheels, and rolled up into wagons, also on wheels! That, of course, rolled up ramps into the train cars -- HOI rail "baggage" cars.

With the folding tables and blue covers that served as our desks, Company Manager Tommy Collins, Gerald "Butch" Collins, and Bob

"My Story" by Carl Moseley

Gaylor were setting up our office, including the two hand-driven typewriters and a couple of old-time mechanical calculators! An office rotary dial phone completed our HOI office!

My immediate job was to acquaint myself, with Bob Gaylor's assistance, with the *Holiday On Ice* system of paying invoices, show payroll, banking of receipts, and the biggie: "boxoffice"! I was familiar with the first items, but, and of most importance, "boxoffice" was a new one on me -- the accounting for **every ticket**, sold or unsold, for **every seat** in the house, and/or cash money for same, for **each performance**! It was highly complicated and had to be right, to the penny -- I'll explain how it worked, later.

My wife Linda's job was to learn each number in the show, one at a time, while being rehearsed solo, afternoons, by Lucy Carpenter, and after a few days in a group rehearsal of the number, after the show. The kids really loved that!

The next performance, she would be in the show! In the meantime, she was to watch the show each performance to learn it all better.

After a night or two, Tommy Colllins told us to take a night off and use his free tickets to see Johnny Mathis, who was performing downtown. We were thrilled and really enjoyed seeing Johnny Mathis perform live!

Guess who showed up during practice ice the next afternoon? Ray Balmer came in the building with Johnny Mathis in tow, and introduced him all around! Then Ray put on his skates and proceeded to show Johnny his huge axel!!

*See color photo section:
Cover of the program for the 1965 Holiday On Ice (U.S.A.)*

Chapter Four
Learning the Ropes

As that first week with *Holiday On Ice* progressed, I began to do the paperwork side of my job, overseen by Bob Gaylor, who would be leaving after the next city, Miami Beach (probably not much to the sorrow of Butch Collins, who had been married to Rosita Percelly). Rosita would be leaving then, also, and Bob & Rosita were soon to be married! We had not had time to purchase a steamer trunk before leaving for the show, and so I took Bob Gaylor's trunk off his hands for a very reasonable amount.

Linda was moving on with rehearsals by Lucy Carpenter, and by Friday night she was ready to rehearse the opening "feather" number with the whole group, after the show, which really enthralled the "kids", I'm sure! Performance Director Anne ("Annie") Schmidt, in calling the rehearsal which had been posted on the show bulletin "Board", didn't seemed too thrilled, though, as she called out Linda's name. I'm not sure exactly why, but have inner thoughts.

"My Story" by Carl Moseley

As time went on, Annie and Linda became good friends, and Annie was very supportive of Linda in a couple of troublesome episodes.

The rehearsal, with recorded music, or maybe with Jim Brimer, show pianist and assistant conductor, playing in his role of rehearsal pianist, went smoothly, and Linda was approved to be in the number for the next performance, a Saturday matinee, if I remember correctly.

When Linda came out of the dressing room the first time, and passed me in full white opening costume, white wig and all, on the way to backstage ice, I was a bit taken aback, to say the least! Up to now rehearsal practice had been with only recorded music. Now she was suddenly going in, in costume and make-up, to skate with a group under performance show lights and to a live orchestra, in front of a live audience.

Not to worry, however -- all went as smooth as the opening ice, and Linda was ready to conquer her next installment of the show.

See color photo section:
Linda Moseley in the HOI'65 opening "Feather" number

A brief video clip of it is available online:
https://www.youtube.com/watch?v=LEaj3vyLIV8

Chapter Five
Taking Care of the Show

Holiday On Ice of 1965 (U.S.A.) finished its Jacksonville engagement successfully, and Sunday night we were on the show train again, and on our way to the next city, Miami Beach!

Morris Chalfen, HOI President (and brother-in law of Tommy Collins and Butch Collins), came in the last day in Jacksonville, and decided to ride the show train with us to Miami Beach. Of course, Tommy was sure that Mr. C got a "bedroom", and didn't need to sleep in an "upper berth" like Jack Lemmon and Marilyn Monroe in *Some Like It Hot*.

Production staff and business meetings were planned for Miami Beach, apparently, as several other execs showed up there, too -- as good a place as any, for meetings, right?

Al Grant ("Silent Al" -- another story, another day!), who was HOI general manager and the man who hired me with Tommy's approval,

"My Story" by Carl Moseley

checked in. Chester Hale and his wife and associate Maureen "came in," and I met them for the first time.

Chester, our principal director/choreographer, assisted by Annie Schmidt up to that time, was a major dance and showbiz personality who had danced in the famous "Ballet Russe de Monte Carlo" and in Pavlova's dance company as her protege. He had directed Ice Capades before HOI, and before that starred as a dancer on Broadway. He had his own ballet studio in New York and directed/choreographed dance numbers in Hollywood movies for the Marx Brothers and "Anna Karanina", etc. Much more about legend Chester Hale, later.

The building we played was the old (new then) Miami Beach Auditorium, home of *The Jackie Gleason Show* during the TV season, but empty when we were there. HOI was actually housed in the convention center extension, next door to Jackie's auditorium "room", which I had to pass through several times a day,. I always said "Hi" to Jackie, as I passed in front of the stage!

More, perhaps, tomorrow, about our Miami Beach stay - pretty factual today; more juicy later, maybe -- not too juicy, however... never want to offend!

I'll leave you, today with one last thought via Morris Chalfen. Mr. C passed me in the auditorium hall early on in Miami Beach, and turned to me and said: "Take care of Holiday On Ice."

I think I always did, and maybe can manage a bit to take some care of the memory of "Holiday," even now... *Thanks, all!*

See color photo section:
Jackie Gleason's auditorium. There was a huge birthday cake,
in flowers, in front, when the author was there.

Chapter Six

From the Ice to the Beach

Where to start? There is so much to say about our *Holiday On Ice* of 1965 (U.S.A.) stay in Miami Beach!

"The Beach Boys" were the next attraction in the building, and a huge banner proclaiming them hung in the lobby, but since we had "left the building" like Elvis by the time they arrived, we never made contact.

The Smothers Brothers were appearing down the street, however, and a bunch of the "kids" went to see them! A lot of the cast was at the Ankara, an older, but nice hotel on the Ocean Highway, but not on the beach side, as was the Saxony across the street

My dad showed up, in transit back to Tampa, from a solo vacation to South America, and renewed acquaintances with Morris Chalfen. He heartedly greeted Mr. C as "Morris", something I never quite dared to do, even when Mr. C dictated a letter to me years later addressed to Skee Goedhart, I believe, in Europe, about the possibility of our getting the Protopopovs, and with Al Grant who my dad also knew when the promoted Ice Vogues & *Holiday On Ice* back in 1947 and 1948.

"My Story" by Carl Moseley

My father, Carl H. Moseley, stayed at the Saxony, of course, but enjoyed watching the show with Linda in a couple more numbers by now.

Bob Gaylor had eased me into the paperwork side of my job, and I had a handle on most of it except the all-important Boxoffice, which was soon to be digested! I had learned how to process the very complicated show payroll, of 100 folks on tour. One hundred or so checks were made out in our Cleveland office, which I signed (co-signed by Tommy Collins) and passed out at intermission on Friday nights.

The basic payroll records were in Cleveland, but each week I had to send big sheets in, with all sorts of changes for any extra work, move-in and out, sewing the set curtain, etc., and extra performances. It was tricky, too, as skaters, musicians, stagehands, and staff (us) were all on different numbers of shows per week for pay purposes!

The exciting news in Miami Beach, was that Ronnie Robertson had been hired to star in the new show the next Fall! I was thrilled, as I had seen Ronnie several times in Ice Capades, live, and also in the 1956 U.S. Championships in Philadelphia against our Ray Balmer (Raymond Blommer) and Hayes and David Jenkins.

What a cast this would make, along with Tommy Allen Weinreich, Jimmy Crockett, and others. Arguably the three fastest spinners in the world would be in the same show the next season!

Madison Square Garden Corporation and ABC/Paramount, the new owners, along with Mr. C who retained a 20% interest and management contract, were beefing up the show for our first New York date in September in the Garden, taking over the dates from Ice Capades.

See Linda Moseley and Terry Cramer Kessler King, Adri Verzaal, & other friends, in HOI'65 online:
https://www.youtube.com/watch?v=g8eQ3cwSG_M

Chapter Seven

The In-Between Times

Alice Quessy LeMac and many others spent lots of idle hours at the pool at the Ankara, but most of my time was spent learning my new job, and getting all the office work side of it organized, and Linda Moseley was occupied learning the rest of the show numbers.

I was in the show office at the Miami Beach Auditorium by around ten each morning, to catch any phone calls or to address any problems that may have arisen, and they often did! Tommy Collins arrived soon after, and Butch, too. Bob Gaylor was still there, helping me, until the end of this run in Miami.

We stayed in the building, office, or thereabouts, with a short lunch break, until 4:00 p.m., or so, at which time on weekdays I would try to put on my skates and get on the open ice, for some practice time.

A few principals often came in about that time too, and others, working on their own skating. Of course, I had to be back at the building by show time (or earlier when I began selling programs at the front door for extra money), and stayed until the Boxoffice report was finished, which I had yet to learn.

"My Story" by Carl Moseley

Skaters had to report in by "Half-Hour," one-half hour before the show started, or one full hour before on opening days.

The ice was open for a while after the show at night, with house lights left on in most places, and a few us often stayed to skate, including, sometimes, Alfredo Mendoza, the "Latin Lover" -- also aptly named!

Alfredo was the premier male water skier in the world during the 1950s and holder of two World Water Skiing Championships. He retired from water skiing and had a second career as a professional show skater, and he was always working on his skating techniques.

If you were nice about asking, Ralph LaVota (later Harris Collins) would run the Zam over the show-chopped-up ice, and make fresh ice for us -- nice and soft, too!!

In Miami Beach, on our three-show Saturday, I took my show-catered Col. Sanders plate, and between the second and third show, I sat down next to Jimmy Crockett to talk with him for the first time.

Jimmy had blown me away when I saw him in the show in Tampa a few weeks earlier. I did not remember him from the previous year, as his presentation had really improved immensely. I thought, "Where did this guy come from?" when I saw Jimmy's nice open Axel, and then a blur spin, close to the caliber of Tommy Allen Weinreich -- an established HOI star performer!

I soon met Marie LaRosk (maybe as we ate Col. Sanders), Jimmy's wife-to-be, and before long Linda and I became good friends with Jimmy and Marie, a friendship that lasted many years.

See color photo section:
Holiday On Ice "hip-swinging, gum-chewing chorines" of the day (actually very fine ensemble skaters), Terry Cramer Kessler King & Olivia Gardner-Hawley

Chapter Eight
Mr. C & the Record Lady

Our *Holiday On Ice* of 1965 engagement in Miami Beach was drawing successfully to a close, and Mr. C (Morris Chalfen), Chester Hale, and other executives were heading home. Morris Chalfen, the man who made *Holiday On Ice* the success it became, was a Minneapolis businessman who also "created" the Lakers professional basketball franchise in Minneapolis and then sold them to LA!

Mr. C had been a partner with Harold Steinman in the hugely successful roller skating show, "Skating Vanities," which featured Ted Shuffle, Michael Meehan, Frank Foster, Doug Breniser, Nancy Lee Parker, Peggy Wallace, Gloria Nord, and others before they switched to ice!

Mr. C grabbed the opportunity to switch gears himself because he had wanted to invest in a major ice show for some time. He backed the Gilbert brothers in Toledo when they needed help to build the necessary additional, portable ice rinks for their fledgling "Holiday On Ice" show, which they "sort of" took out on tour in 1944. (The Gilberts had gained refrigeration experience from their fleet of sandwich wagons.)

"My Story" by Carl Moseley

Morris Chalfen came to their rescue, sold his interest in Skating Vanities, and provided the Gilberts with the funds to build the additional rinks, as well as to enhance production values in every way, and to put a full scale ice show on the road in 1945.

All the cities that had yearned for an ice show such as "Ice Follies" or "Ice Capades" due to lack of ice now had another option with a show that provided its own ice. For his investment, Mr. C became President, and the guiding force, of the new Holiday On Ice Shows, Inc., and the rest, as they say, is history!

Skating Vanities had been produced with the guidance of Radio City Music Hall folks, some of whom moved over to *Holiday On Ice*. One of these transfers was Dolores Pallet, HOI Music Producer, otherwise known as "The Record Lady," but not to her face.

Dolores was very knowledgeable musically, having been rehearsal pianist for the original "Roxy," S.L. Rothafel, who created the "Roxyettes" at the Roxy Theatre, later moving them to Radio City Music Hall and renaming them "The Rockettes." Dolores assisted HOI orchestra conductor and arranger Ben Stabler in selecting and arranging music for the new show each year during rehearsals in Knoxville, Tennessee. The next Fall, Dolores sent Don Watson and me to a music shop in Knoxville to secure records with the songs and classical pieces she and Benny were working on.

I recall something Tommy Collins told me the first week with the show: "No matter what anybody says, don't let it bother you!" I never let it because I never had to. I toured with the most friendly group of touring "show folks." Tommy would always say, "We're not businessmen, we're show folks!" Tommy meant that with 100 people travelling together all the time, in close proximity, things could get a bit hairy at times (and occasionally they did), but I managed to side-step most of the issues.

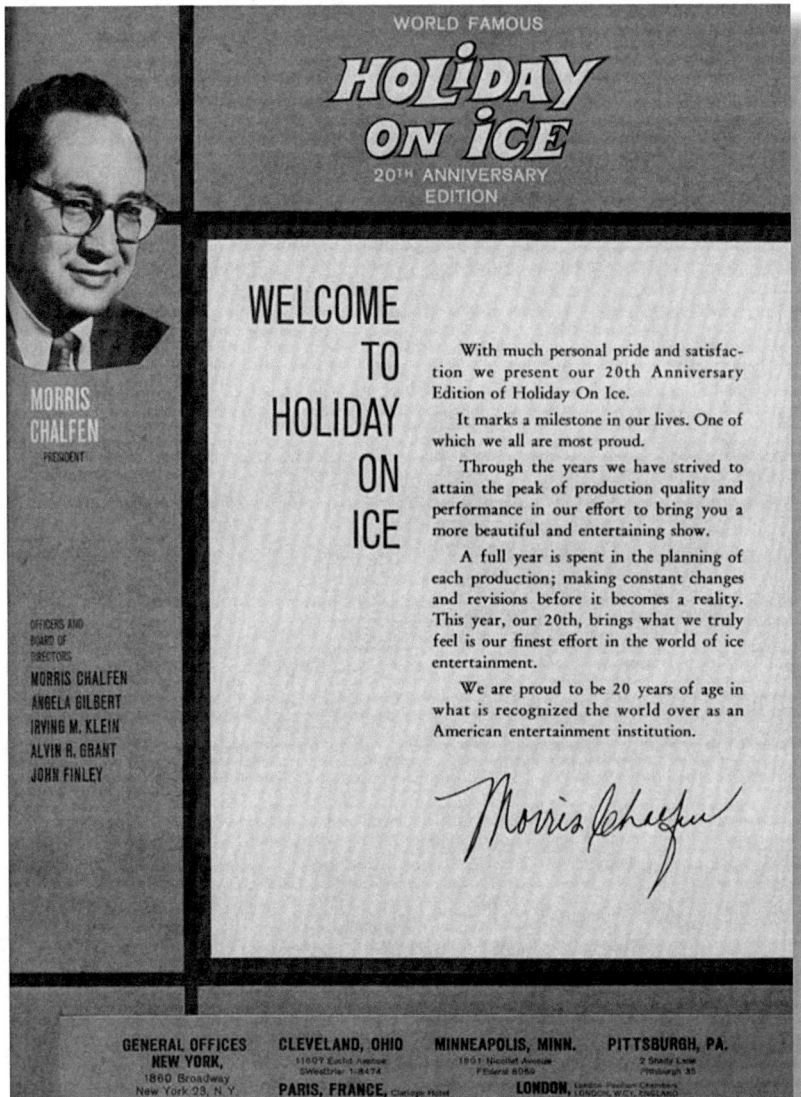

Morris Chalfen letter in HOI program

"My Story" by Carl Moseley

Chapter Nine
Show Train & Party Cars

Before we leave Miami Beach and the original Lum's, where I had fresh squeezed orange juice and fantastic "huevos rancheros" many mornings, I must mention two other skaters. A fine competitive pair, Ron Basten and Chickie Berlin, auditioned in Miami and were hired to join us in the Fall in the chorus, but also as potential understudies, at rehearsals in Knoxville, Tennessee.

After joining, Ron knuckled down to anything assigned to him, chorus-wise or other, and continued to hone his skating skills, resulting in a very successful career with *Holiday On Ice*. He also appeared in a shadow pair feature with Mike Burns, part of which can be seen in the video of *Holiday On Ice* of 1971, on the *Ed Sullivan Show*!

The time came to board the train for the overnight trip to our next city, Jackson, Mississippi. The "James Meredith March Against Fear" in Jackson came the following year (1966) -- one of many marches during that time period to promote black voter registration and bring attention to racism.

Our Pullman cars were made up, beds ready when we arrived at the train, by porters who were familiar with the show cars. That did not stop the parties that commenced in the two "party cars," as we just sat on top of the made-up beds, in lower berths ("lowers"), and/or in "bedrooms" and "staterooms." The third "quiet" car was for mainly married folks and tired stagehands (after working the "out"), but Linda and I managed to have a few semi-quiet gatherings in our bedroom, next to Alice, Joe, and Ronny LeMac.

If we began to disturb Alice, we would just hot-foot it down to the "party" car and someone would shove over in a "lower" to make room (for about three in each, facing three more across the aisle). We had the routine down pretty well by now, and would help make sure there was enough ice, in a lavatory, for mixing water with suds from "the baby" which all shared.

Our *Holiday On Ice* special show train consisted of our three Pullman "sleeper" cars, our three HOI "baggage" cars, an additional boxcar (later), and the engine. Sometimes on our special show runs, the engineer would get a little carried away to make up time, and the train would begin to rock back and forth, from side to side. Stage Manager Joe LeMac was a little paranoid about this, and he would scurry up to the engine and tell the engineer to "Slow Down!"

On good (mainly longer) trips, our Pullman cars, and sometimes all, would be hooked onto a "regular run" train, and we would have the luxury of a lounge car, maybe complete with bar, and on really good runs, man-oh-man, a diner, too!

We always had fun in spite of a few incidents we'll describe later, and we made the best of every situation, as show-folk buds!

Lum's Original Restaurant

Chapter Ten
A Few Snags

Our *Holiday On Ice* of 1965 (U.S.A.) stay in Jackson, Mississippi was rather smooth and uneventful, except for a couple of incidents, below.

We played the new Mississippi Coliseum, described by Wikipedia as "(A) 6,500-seat multipurpose arena in Jackson, Mississippi, built in 1962 and located on the Mississippi State Fairgrounds complex. It sits 2900 feet (884 meters) atop the extinct Jackson Volcano." Yes, volcano!

One of our electricians (who shall remain nameless) was thrown in jail for allegedly failing to pay child support, and his skater girlfriend came into the show office, frantic about it. I don't recall the details, but I think we somehow got him released to rejoin us.

There was a similar incident later, in Detroit, when Tommy Collins was out of town. I had to bail out and go to court to arrange for the release of Lucien LaCroix, of all people, who had been entrapped in a local vice-squad sting!

The other snag was a spike to Linda Moseley's leg, in a spill while were were skating after the show. I am kinda' fuzzy about the city this happened in, but it seems to me that it must have been Jackson, as it was early in our first tour. I do remember that Lucy Carpenter, driven by her helpful boyfriend, took us to an ER for stitches, cautioning Linda to say to the Doc that it happened during rehearsal for the show, rather than skating or practicing on her own, as show insurance would not apply. There were medical insurance issues, even then!

The train for New Orleans left mid-day, at 1:00 p.m., so we gathered in the bar of the hotel that morning, after having to check out of our rooms, and I was introduced to oysters on the half-shell. And let me tell you, they were GOOD, in Jackson, Mississippi! Ralph LaVota offered me one to try, but by the time we boarded the show train I had downed three dozen raw oysters on the half-shell, helped, of course, by beer and cocktail sauce... It makes my mouth water, even now!

"My Story" by Carl Moseley

ALICE QUESSY...
A beauteous redhead with acres of talent. One of icedom's most accomplished performers with a flair for enthralling an audience from the moment she puts her skates to ice. Her versatility includes baton twirling, piano playing, dramatics and a thorough knowledge of dance. At home equally on stage or ice, she has performed in many of the country's theaters as well as its ice arenas. She was one of the first American ice stars to perform in Moscow when Holiday went there under the Cultural Exchange program of the State Department. In spite of the great demand of her profession she manages to find time to raise her two young sons in her home in Clearwater, Fla.

RAY BALMER...
This handsome young man born in Milwaukee, Wisc., is one of the most powerful skaters in the ice world today. His many hours of practice every day plus his devotion to body building has developed extremely strong leg muscles that allow him to attain heights of four to five feet in his exciting jumps. Midwestern Champion in 1954, Eastern Champion in 1955. He was chosen as an alternate on the Olympic & World Teams in 1956. The lure of the travelling show was too much so he joined Holiday in 1957 and has performed with the company since then. When the time comes to hang up his blades for good he plans on entering the real estate profession in his home town of San Diego, California.

HANNA EIGEL...
Lovely Hanna is one of Austria's most famous skaters. Her list of championships is long. And most notable of the titles she holds is, European Champion twice. Second to the incomparable Carol Heiss in the World's Championship in 1957; she was named Austria's Sportswoman of the year. Just when it seemed she was headed for championship honors in every competition, she decided to turn professional with the Vienna Ice Revue. After five years with that show, an offer by Morris Chalfen, President of Holiday On Ice, to tour with his American company, was too difficult to resist. Europe's loss was America's gain and this lovely blonde miss has thrilled audiences from coast to coast.

ALFREDO MENDOZA...
Handsome Alfredo Mendoza is one of the finest all around athletes in the company. Twice world champion water skier and recognized as one of the foremost authorities on the sport. After seeing a performance of Holiday in Tampa he decided he wanted to skate with the show. He bought a pair of skates and carried them all over the world, and would travel hundreds of miles just to find a rink upon which he could practice. He auditioned a few years later and was accepted — starting as a line skater, he practiced morning and night, before and after each show until he had literally raised himself to a starring role, and he is now recognized as one of the finest adagio and show skaters in the world.

JUANITA PERCELLY...
Cute and bubbly Juanita has been in show business all her young life. Literally born backstage, she comes from a famous European circus family. She introduction to the world of ice came while she was working in the family act with the European edition of Holiday. Her father insisted that she learn to skate, and she did. She has turned into one of the strongest and fastest skaters around. Her pair with Tommy Allen is a constant chase for him, but she says, "we have a ball doing the act". Born in Frankfurt, Germany, she speaks 4 languages. She has determined not to follow the family tradition of show business. Her heart is set upon studying cosmetology and hair dressing in Paris and then opening a chic shop in America.

JANE MORRIS...
This exquisite and perfectly proportioned (34-22-34) young blonde is Georgia's gift to Holiday On Ice. Miss Georgia of 1957 and a finalist in the Miss America pageant. Janie has developed into one of the most gifted adagio skaters in the country. She turned to skating as a means of keeping physically fit while reining as the official ambassador of good will for the State of Georgia. Her instructor had her audition for the show while it was in Atlanta and she was signed. Starting as a ballet girl she advanced rapidly into semi feature and feature roles, and now is a full fledged adagio skater. She recalls as her greatest thrill, her attendance at Miss Georgia at the second inaugural ball for President Eisenhower and his stopping to shake her hand. Who wouldn't? Stop to shake hands with Janie, we mean...

TOMMY ALLEN...
In his seventh year with Holiday is recognized as one of the finest show skaters around. His remarkable ability to spin at a dizzying speed has earned him the title of "Whirling Dervish". A gold medalist, the highest award a skater can earn, he is an avid sports fan being an accomplished equestrian, swimmer and skier. He lives with his family in Las Cruces, New Mexico where his Dad is an automobile dealer. He loves the life he leads and intends to keep on skating for a long time before retiring to the family business.

SANDY WIRWILL...
Sandy is the "baby" of the show... A pert and cute teen age miss from Dearborn, Michigan. Although she had been skating for a number of years she had never seen a professional ice show until she was taken by relatives to see "Holiday On Ice". She returned home with the ambition to become an ice star. She studied hard and two years later auditioned and was accepted. She loves travelling and has the desire to stay with the show as long as she can still glide around the ice. She is a collector of statues, abstracts and jewelry. Crazy about shoes and buys at least one pair in every city.

DEELEY & LEECH...
Ted Deeley and Johnny Leech, two individual and funny comedians met six years ago and pooled their talents into one of the funniest acts in the world of ice show business. Their contrasting styles coordinate perfectly for a melange of fun and frolic. Johnny designs and builds most of the props for their act; Ted is the idea man... Serious students of human nature, they feel that comedy takken from everyday life is the funniest, and they are so right.

HAMI BROWN...
This zany Scotsman has performed his act in practically every country in the world and always obtains the same result, long, loud laughter, which proves that pantomine comedy on ice is a universal language, understood by one and all. An ex-hockey player, Hami decided it would be more fun to fall on purpose than to be knocked down purposely. Making people laugh is his career, and one at which he works with great success.

THE BRUISES...
These riotous clowns, Noble Rochester, Johnny Leech and Hami Brown would do anything for a laugh, and do! Although they take many hard bumps and falls during the course of their performance, the experience of years has perfected their timing to the point that they do so in relative safety. One of the most famous of all ice show comedy acts, The Scrubwomen originated when one late evening when they were rehearsing in Wembly, England, they saw one of the arena's charwomen try the ice not knowing the boys were watching. They translated her amateurish attempts into what has now become the classic comedy routine on ice.

THE PEACOCKS...
Jimmy and Mary Peacock are twenty year veterans of the ice show business. Their home is in Brighton, England and they have skated in virtually every country in the world. Their act is truly a novelty in that it was conceived, and built by Jimmy, and his "Three Legged Man" has never been performed by anyone other than himself. Although they enjoy their travelling about the world and wouldn't have it any other way, they do enjoy spending vacations at home in England where they indulge in the everyday pursuits of the homeowner, gardening, painting, decorating and gabbing with friends and neighbors, except this is a Holiday for them.

HOUN' DAWG...
Houn' Dawg has just recently returned to the show after an involuntary retirement. Producer Ruth Tyson decided that Houn' Dawg had seen enough service with the show and was entitled to some rest, so she retired the number. She didn't reckon with the Houn' Dawg fan clubs, and each season that "Houn' Dawg" did not appear, letters would pour into the offices from all over the country asking why "Houn' Dawg" was not in the show. Last year she acceded to public demand and put him back in. This year he's back bigger and better than ever and the fans are glad. Incidentally, just between us Houn' Dawg is really Alfredo Mendoza and Johnny Ladue. We're not sure they're happy, as they say it's warm in there.

Holiday On Ice 1965 program page describing our fine HOI stars

Chapter Eleven
Deadwood

Before I found out how much I loved the oysters in Jackson, Company Manager Tommy Collins had begun taking me with him each time he went to check the "boxoffice"... *mui importante!*

The "boxoffice" was the financial heart of things and what HOI depended upon for its very survival. I began to understand what Morris Chalfen had meant in Miami Beach when he said to me: "Take care of *Holiday On Ice.*"

After intermission of each performance, the local building box office manager would call and say he was ready for us to check the receipts for that performance. Tommy and I would then go to the box office and take a look. Each time, there had be either an amount of money, or unsold tickets (and passes), to account for every seat in the house.

This was in the days of the rectangular tickets, which were supplied in blocks, and the unsold numbered tickets (blocks) were called "Deadwood." The cash receipts number plus the value of the deadwood (and passes) had to equal what a sold-out house (called "Going Clean"), would have provided! The Deadwood was stacked on a table for us to re-count, along with the passes. We would go back to our show office with the gross numbers, and Tommy - soon me - would do a full box-office report, with seats and prices, on our own HOI show forms.

Once finished, with the math reported on a Woodstock typewriter, we would call the box office, once more, to see if our final numbers matched - if not, it was back down there, again until they did agree!

One would think that this was a pretty fool-proof way of making sure that no one was skimming off ticket sales money, and that HOI was getting what it earned, but believe it or not, Tommy told me that there had been instances on the past of people, building and/or box office managers, even having their own identical sets of tickets printed, to sub some in, as "Deadwood", and pocket a bundle of cash.
   -- *"Figures don't lie, but liars figure"!*

HOI'65 program page with the folks that made Holiday On Ice succeed for many years

Chapter Twelve
Rat Holes & Jewel Boxes

Our next city, with *Holiday On Ice* of 1965 (U.S.A.) was, if I remember correctly, New Orleans. We were getting close to jumping off for our 30-day stay in Mexico City, and Tommy Collins took me to Mexican Consulate offices in the World Trade Center in New Orleans to smooth out details for our train border crossing at Laredo, Texas into Nuevo Laredo, Mexico.

We collected all personnel passports to have them checked out before the actual show train crossing in order to expedite the process. I also compiled a huge roster of cast members, stagehands and all, with birth dates, home cities, etc., which we submitted for perusal.

Well, it was our first time in New Orleans, a really fun city, and although we took in all the sights and night spots we could absorb, in order to conserve funds we followed the action of Annie Schmidt. Annie always knew the places that cost less, and checked into joint rooms (with a common bathroom in-between), with Mike and Terry Kessler (Terry Cramer Kessler King). It turned out to be pretty much, for want of a better description, a rat-hole of a hotel!

There were peep holes in the doors, and once on boarding the shaky elevator, which Annie was on, too, I was greeted by a poor old dirty fellow, looking like he had just been beaten up, with blood here and there! I think they tore down that hotel before we arrived the next year, and thankfully, we stayed in a new "jewel-box" of a motel.

This first year we persevered, and we did manage to have a fun time in New Orleans, hitting new spots each night, in the Vieux Carré, which never closes! I was hoping to go to the famous French restaurant, Antoine's, but we could not get reservations (we did visit it years later).

Not to worry... Mike Kessler found us a nice table at another fine French restaurant, Arnoud's and we enjoyed dining there, having a superb repast with Mike and Terry.

See color photo section:
HOI'65 -- our lovely, lovely, show gals, all fondly remembered!

Chapter Thirteen
The Ins and Outs

While in New Orleans, with *Holiday On Ice* of 1965 (U.S.A.), we took in all of the night spots, from Pat O'Brien's, with the gals playing and singing on twin grand pianos and the huge free punch glasses you got to keep as souvenirs, to small quiet pubs with bowls of roasted peanuts on the bar and the floors covered with peanut shells!

On the day we went to the Mexican Consulate, Tommy Collins had me meet him for an eggs benedict brunch at "The Court Of The Two Sisters," a lovely place in a hidden courtyard with overhanging oaks, if I remember correctly! A couple of other times, it was just at "White Castle"!

HOI General Manager Al Grant had asked Tommy if I had become familiar with the working of the "in's" and the "out's" yet, so Tommy took me down to the rail siding where our HOI baggage cars were parked to observe the loading of our HOI wagons into the train cars on closing night.

Our "baggage car crew" consisted then of Ralph LaVota, Gene Theslof, Jr., Todd Schoomaker, Butch Collins, Frank Micale, and Jim (Hoss)

Coatney. (Later, beginning in Knoxville, I joined the crew for extra money.)

Immediately at 8:00 p.m., Sunday (closing) night (all legitimate theaters went "dark" on Sunday evenings), the local stagehands would begin loading all the show equipment onto our 19 custom built HOI wagons, bringing the wagons into the building from where they had been parked in back, some out onto the ice for easier loading.

Soon the overhead beams and set beams would be lowered, too, for dismantling the overhead lights, and the set curtains, backdrops, and lights. Most everything, except long steel beams, and a few odd props, fit into custom-made crates on casters, for rolling into the wagons, which rolled, pushed by the jeeps, up ramps, into the long tunnels formed by our end-to-end three baggage cars. These were dining cars that had been reamed out to their metal skin by Gene Verchesky in Venice, Florida, who did same for Ice Capades and Ringling Bros.

Our baggage car crew, above, with our jeeps, hauled each filled wagon from the building to the rail siding, where the jeep, again, would push the wagon up the ramp and into the rail cars, guided in front of the wagon by another crew member, walking backwards, guiding with the big "tongue bar" attached to the wagon's two front wheels.

At the last minute, before reaching the back of the wagons already in the train tunnel, this guiding fellow would throw the tongue bar up into a clamp, on the front of the wagon, and step aside into the few inches on the car side as the wagons banged together -- pretty tricky! Years later, our Wagon Master Jules Mayeur didn't throw the tongue bar quickly enough, and it stuck right through him! Ouch! But Jules survived, somehow, to tell the story another day.

See color photo section:
HOI '65 Stars

Chapter Fourteen

A Venerable Venue

The building we played in New Orleans, the New Orleans Municipal Auditorium, was built in 1930. It is a venerable historic structure, just on the edge of the French Quarter.

The show looked great there, as the audience seating climbed rather quickly on each side, and the audience was more up close than in some venues. It was decorated ornately on the inside, and the only drawbacks were that, although it had air conditioning, after a fashion, we had to pay extra when the AC was on. We pretty much limited the AC to performance times, making our show office rather uncomfortable in May!

The Auditorium had no ice, so we had to put in our own ice. Usually this is not a problem, and the ice was okay for HOI '65.

A couple of years later, part of the Mardi Gras celebration was held in the building just before our engagement, so our ice engineers were delayed in putting the rink down, which led to ice problems. We even brought in crushed ice to fill in, and dry ice to help freeze, and the ice was still a wreck the first night.

Going back, Ice Capades had its very first performances in this building in June of 1940 according to Wikipedia. I'll never know how, as large portable rinks were unheard of that early, to my knowledge. HOI's were first built in 1944, and AC?

Wikipedia reports: "Ice Capades' first performance was four months after its founding, on June 16, 1940, at New Orleans Municipal Auditorium. The show closed there on June 29 and moved to Atlantic City Convention Hall, where it played nightly from July 19 through September 2. Famous skaters in the large cast included Belita, Robin Lee and Vera Hruba. The group's first touring season under the Ice Capades name covered 24 cities between November 1940 and May 1941."

Nate Walley joined us in New Orleans, that year, I believe, and stayed with us through Mexico City, before going to Europe and the HOI shows there. Nate was Director of Figure Skating for Holiday On Ice, worldwide, and circulated between all shows, working with principals. Actually, any hard-working skater sought him out in order to improve for advancement. Nate, the "spin doctor" among his other areas of expertise, was very helpful to many!

In his Ice Capades days, Nate and Robert Dench had been instrumental in Alan Konrad's ("The Ghost of the Arena") legendary climb from chorus skater to long-time star performer! Nate would come into our show office, and loved to chat about his famous daughter Deborah Walley, the first "Gidget" of the movies!

New Orleans Municipal Auditorium

"My Story" by Carl Moseley

Chapter Fifteen

Hooray for the Ice Engineers

After a successful stay in New Orleans, we, *Holiday On Ice* of 1965, moved on to Mobile, Alabama, our last stop before Mexico City!

We played a beautiful new building in Mobile, the Municipal Auditorium, which *Holiday On Ice* had "opened" the year before. According to Wikipedia: "The structure opened as the Mobile Municipal Auditorium on July 9, 1964. It celebrated its opening with a "Holiday on Ice" ice skating show. It was built with the city's longtime Mardi Gras celebrations in mind. The concourse area is often used for balls during Mardi Gras."

Mardi Gras, there, had just finished, and there were still scraps of paper decorations strewn around in some of the rooms, including our HOI office room. Beautiful as it was, the Auditorium had no permanent ice, and our ice engineers, Bobby Johnson and Verne Britton, had leap-frogged HOI's second portable ice unit ahead of us.

The HOI portable rinks were transported on truck trailers, one with the large refrigeration units -- compressors, condenser, and brine chiller, and another for all the pipe sections, 30' x 4' sections, then, of one-and-one-quarter inch steel pipe that made up the ice floor grid.

Verne or Bobby, depending on which city, would arrive several days ahead of us, and pick up a local group of laborers to install the ice. They began about two days before our opening, by laying a "vapor barrier" of visqueen (plastic sheeting), or tar paper on the building floor, and then the pipe grid sections would be laid down to form a rink 60' by 120' (or 140'), with 4" or so "header" pipes on each side for "supply" and "return" of the 19 degree or so calcium chloride brine solution, pumped through them from the brine chiller on the refrigeration truck out back. The name "headers" came from the wooden covers, with lights, that originally covered these big pipes.

Before the pumping began, the space between the pipes in the grid had to be filled with a mixture of sand and sawdust and then leveled to the tip top of the pipes. Back in 1947, when I was 13, I had helped to wheelbarrow the sawdust into my dad's building, the Coliseum, for Ice Vogues in Tampa.

Once the brine was flowing, and the grid was cold enough, Bobby or Verne would, by hand, use a light spray of water to form the first ice crust, which would soon be hand-sprayed again with white water-base paint. The spraying would continue, over and over, heavier and heavier, until there was about 1/2" of new ice, all ready for *Holiday On Ice*!

Ted Deeley, in his solo routine on his pics and heels for a time, did a pretty good job of chopping up a small section of ice, right up front, and about my first day with the show, Ray Balmer came marching into our show office, in costume, after just finishing his number, to complain to Tommy Collins that Ted had once again chopped up the ice right in the landing area for Ray's big axel... welcome to "Showbiz"!

The Mobile Municipal Auditorium

"My Story" by Carl Moseley

HOI'65 Characters & Novelty Acts

Holiday On Ice 1965 U.S.A.

Mexico

Chapter Sixteen

Heading South of the Border

A lot of my time in Mobile (my mother was from there, originally) was spent in preparation for the big move the following week to Mexico City, Mexico D.F. (Departemento Federale), for a 30-day stay, playing the Arena Mexico.

I settled with our ice engineers, their detailed expense sheets, labor and all, for the last portable few portable ice engagements, and continued to finalize the paperwork needed for the border crossing into Mexico. At the border, the show personnel would change to Mexican Pullman (sleeper) cars, but our HOI equipment "baggage" cars would continue on, hooked onto the Mexican train that met us at the border.

Our rail cars were subject to inspection by Mexican immigration officials, but, in reality, there was no way our HOI wagons could have been unloaded, mid-trip, without our crew, and it would have caused a huge delay. Tommy Collins wanted to take a full case of U.S. Black & White Scotch, which was expensive in Mexico, down for our Mexican promoter Jauquin Guerra, and a few other baubles the inspectors might interfere with.

"My Story" by Carl Moseley

Just in case, we had Jim (Hoss) Coatney, our wagon master, weld a false bottom in the Zamboni snow bin, under which the Scotch and other precious items were placed, believe it or not!

It was a three-day train trip to Mexico City -- around the top of the Gulf, down through Texas to Laredo, and then on down to Mexico City -- one night in U.S. Pullman cars and one night in the Mexican sleeper cars.

Tommy Collins and I flew down ahead of the train to clear last minute immigration details at the border. We flew on four planes that trip -- Mobile to New Orleans to Dallas to San Antonio to Laredo, the last on a four-seater "crop duster" type plane, with Tommy sitting next to the pilot, and me in the back biting my nails, and looking straight down from the plastic window!

The pilot followed the highway below and set us down on a dirt runway (with tumbleweeds blowing across it), and an airport guy on a hand-held mike, lodged in a wooden shack, guiding him in! We were to stay that night, awaiting the show train, in a first class spiffy motel, complete with pool, Tex-Mex restaurant, and all, right on the Rio Grande, next to the highway and foot bridge, and across the border from Laredo to Nuevo Laredo.

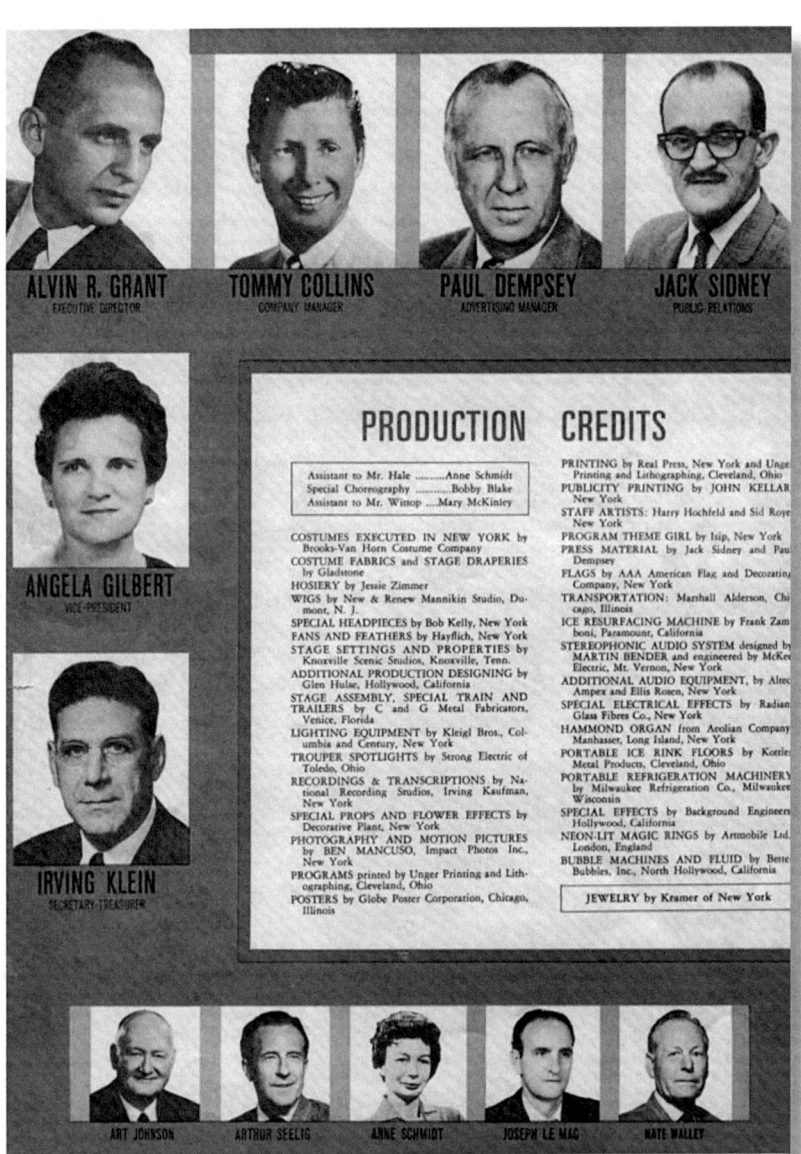

HOI'65 program page with the folks that made Holiday On Ice succeed for many years

Chapter Seventeen

Scotch & A Swim

After landing on that dirt strip runway in Laredo, Texas, *Holiday On Ice* of 1965 Company Manager Tommy Collins and I made our way to the office of our HOI border agent, Dan Hastings, near the railway station and the crossing area.

Dan was an American of Mexican heritage who spoke fluent Spanish and English, and his business was representing many American companies to facilitate movement of products, etc., back and forth to Mexico. After a hearty greeting by Dan, he broke out the Scotch from a little fridge next to his desk, and we all had a well-earned refresher, as we turned over Tommy's briefcase full of passports, shot records, and other paperwork.

Dan would preview all the paperwork with Mexican border officials before the show train arrived, at which time each of the show personnel would get his/her passport back, and shot records, to present to a Doc, on boarding the Mexican section of our train.

Business settled, for the moment, Dan then took us for a ride to see some of the new sights in Nuevo Laredo, Mexico. Dan dropped us off at our spiffy Laredo hotel, La Posada, where Tommy and I were to spend the night, awaiting the HOI show train's arrival the next day.

After checking into our spacious room, Tommy ordered ice and a bottle of Scotch from room service, and we retired, refreshers in hand, to the inviting hotel pool! Butch Collins' girlfriend, Paula Seeman, was there ahead of Butch, and we all had a fun swim, with some water fights between Tommy and Paula.

The hotel was right next to the International (highway) Bridge, and that evening Tommy Collins and I moseyed over, on foot, to check out a couple of the close-by nightspots for some beer and light entertainment, mariachis, etc. On crossing the bridge, we encountered little Mexican boys, attempting to sell chicklets, and on the way back across, some of the same little boys were curled up, sleeping, on the bridge.

The historic, resort-like La Posada Hotel on the banks of the Rio Grande in Laredo, Texas after completing an extensive $15 million makeover that combined the hotel's historic Spanish influence and colonial architecture

Chapter Eighteen
The Crossing

After a good night's sleep at our luxurious hotel, and a nice huevos rancheros breakfast on the hotel outside patio, Tommy and I made our way to the office of Dan Hastings, our U.S. travel representative, and on to the railway station with Dan. Our U.S. Pullman passenger cars would be left at the border, and everybody would switch to Mexican Pullman cars, for the last half day and night on the train, as part of a Mexican passenger train.

Our show equipment "baggage" cars were hooked onto this Mexican train there, too. The Mexican Pullman cars were similar to U.S. (many having been purchased from a U.S. railway), and were nice enough, although not quite as up-to-date, and with rather iffy AC! On a positive note, there was a club car on the end, to our relief, and in which all seats were kept occupied by HOI folks! I think I remember a diner on this train, too...

My widowed aunt, Edith Brown, from Rome, GA, wanted to go to Mexico City with us, and it was nice to see her, and my wife at the time, Linda, as I boarded the train for the last half day and night and day on the train!

On boarding the Mexican cars, everyone got their passports and shot records back, which were individually perused by a Mexican doc, one at a time. The immigration paperwork we had turned over to Dan Hastings the day before included a handful of white envelopes holding a few hundred U.S. dollars to purchase additional oil for the train wheels (ahem), which seemed to be moving very smoothly, as we shortly pulled out of the station, and on to Mexico City!

This Mexican passenger train made quite a few brief stops along the way at picturesque, small villages, as it made its way across the Mexican desert terrain, cactus and all, and there were vendors by the train at each stop selling blankets, beads, and jewelry to whomever wished to hop off, briefly for a leg stretch.

Mexican passenger train and club car

Chapter Nineteen

The Little Engine That Could

My wife, Linda, and my Aunt, Edith Brown, had already been on the train for a day and a night, of the two-night, three-day trip, as had some of our new friends, Mike and Terry Cramer Kessler King, possibly Colleen Erb, and, I believe, Jimmy Crockett and Marie LaRosk.

As we had quite some time to go, we converged on the club car to socialize, take in the sights the train passed, play cards, soak up cervesas, etc. "Dos mas Cervesas, por favor!"

The desert sights were many, and the train would stop often, briefly, by small adobe villages, where one could get off, for a leg stretch, and maybe a purchase from one of the Mexican vendors, who met the train.

The next day began to stretch out, however, as we finally left the desert and began our climb to Mexico City. It is located in the Valley of Mexico (Valle de México), a large valley (on a dried-up lake bed) in the high plateaus at the center of Mexico, at an altitude of 7,350 ft.
As the train trudged higher on our approach to Mexico City, it moved

more and more slowly, and I began to wonder whether the "little engine that could" *could* make it to the high plateau. It proved its worth, however, and late in the day, travel-weary *Holiday On Ice* gypsies sighed as it finally pulled into the station of Mexico City. Mexican cabs awaited us to take each and all to our four hotels of choice.

Vendor with her wares beside the tracks

The train frequently stopped by small villages for a leg stretch and shopping with Mexican vendors

Chapter Twenty

Sights and Sounds and Castinets

Mexico City, our final stop for *Holiday On Ice* of 1965 (U.S.A.), had the Most to offer of interest of any city on the tour, except perhaps New York City.

We did 50 shows in 30 days! That was about 350 costume changes for the "kids". We "went clean" (complete sell out) the whole last week including a "six-pack" (last two days, each three shows).

There was no end to the sights & attractions in this huge multi-million population city, and we tried to cover as many as possible, from Chapultepec Park and Lake, and the Emperor's Palace, to the University of Mexico, the Folklorico Ballet, and a small club where you drank wine from cloth sacks and watched supreme guitarists and singers on a darkened stage in the center. On occasion, at the Arena Mexico, a group of mariachis would take the ice and entertain!

There were plenty of fine restaurants, too, from the Villa Fontana, with its strolling violinists, to Delmonico's, which was close to our hotel so there were several visits. It featured flown-in Western beef, a dining room with a waterfall covering one wall, and three tiers of waiters, each livery attired separately, and the cocktail waiter making your super dry martini, at your table, with a frosted glass out of his little fridge and adding just a drop of vermouth from an eye-dropper. There was no reason to complain about lack of food, there, but it was a bit pricy, for some.

We checked into our hotel recommended by Tommy Collins, the Golden Suites, in the center of the tourist district, and within walking distance, if necessary, from the Arena Mexico. It was four stories, with eight apartments, two on each floor, front and back. We were on the third floor in front, with Tommy and Janie just below. Alice, Joe, and Ronny LeMac were just above us, and through the big open screenless windows, we could hear Alice Quessy above, practicing on the castinets for her number "Rio Rita" the following year -- she played them live, as she skated! There was no AC, but the weather was rather pleasant (except for frequently foul air) and cool enough, with windows open at night.

Hanna Eigel & Hami Brown were at the Golden Suites, too, as I remember. The bulk of the HOI folks paired up for apartments and rooms at another nice, but less expensive hotel, the historic La Casa de La Luna.

Arena Mexico

La Casa de la Luna

"My Story" by Carl Moseley

Chapter Twenty-One
El Spectacle Holiday

Well, after two nights and three days of train travel, we finally got the show unloaded and set up, and we opened in Mexico City to a sell-out crowd! They loved "El Spectacle Holiday," and every time we would leave, out back, to take busses between shows to the "Chalet Suizo," the throngs of crowds would be waiting there, programs in hand, for autographs by all!

The Chalet Suizo (Swiss) served a nice change from the Mexican menu, so we contracted with them to reserve a dining room for our cast between shows on three-show and two-show days. The show paid for meals, and skaters paid for wine or beer. The food was excellent!

I was in Mexico for three HOI tours, so I will relay happenings from each, as seems timely. I was not doing the in's and out's this first time there, but on our second trip to Mexico City, an interesting thing happened.

First, in order to unload the long rail baggage car tunnel, the cars had to be arranged, at destination, opposite to when they were loaded, so that the last things in, the three jeeps and the Zamboni, could come out first, to pull the wagons out one at a time. Well, somehow the Mexican railway had erred, and when the "baggage car crew" arrived at the rail siding, there our cars sat, turned the WRONG way! This slowed us down just a bit, but proved fun and exposure to great sights. Don Watson and I just hopped on the "cow catcher" on the front of the engine and rode it all the way outside of the main city rail yards to a "Y" where the cars could be reversed!

We saw lots of eye-opening things on that ride, such as the long twists of bare wire connected together that stretched from tin roof shacks (each with a TV antenna) up to a power pole to siphon off electric juice. Wouldn't want to be there in a rainstorm!

On the fun side of our first stay, Tommy Collins was acquainted with the young owner of both the Delmonico's and Mauna Loa restaurants. I think this fellow might had had a thing for Janie, who in any case, invited a group of about twelve of us to a splendid repast, with a huge selection of all the best island dishes put before us, at the Mauna Loa!

Pictured here is the owner's wife and Hanna Eigel, Janie Morris, Lucy Carpenter, and Linda Moseley sipping on a deadly concoction that day, with Joe Easton smiling on!

The Mauna Loa was no longer there when we returned the next year, as it had burned to the ground!

"My Story" by Carl Moseley

Chapter Twenty-Two
A Bit of Fun Filling In

Settled in for a long engagement (the last on the tour), many turned to taking in the numerous sights offered in Mexico City. As assistant company manager, paperwork and reports consumed many of my daylight hours, compounded by the fact that there was really no good place in the Arena Mexico for our show office, and Tommy Collins set it up in his hotel apartment at The Golden Suites.

So, although I was always in the building for the show, the reports, etc. had to wait for another day. Linda and my visiting aunt, Edith Brown, took an enjoyable day excursion by a tourist taxi to the pyramids 30 miles out -- the ruins of pre-Columbian Teotihuacan. Tourists were encouraged to mount the fully intact "Pyramid of the Sun" for a stunning bird's eye view over all that remains of the once bustling city.

Not too much ice time for me during that first Mexico City stay. One late afternoon, however, I was on the ice messing around with Ray Balmer's music playing on my little cassette player, and someone wandered in. I was working on hitting an axel at a music peak, as Ray did, and I was asked if I were going to go in for Ray closing night, as part of the many gags that occurred in that last show of the year. No way -- for the record, I never got even close to the ice, on closing night, consumed as I was with my typewriter and calculator in a corner niche, working on final 50-show settlement reports, in both pesos and dollars!

The next year, however, Don Watson and I hit the almost vacant ice at the Arena Mexico many late afternoons, after which we walked back to our hotels, stopping along the way for a couple of cool margaritas in the lobby of the Hilton Hotel.

During that second year, I hung out quite a bit in Guy Longpre and Ivor Robson's large dressing room, and I kept my skate bag there. Guy and Ivor asked if I would like to do Guy's "Sailor" number with them as a lark and time-filler. They rehearsed me a couple of times in their dressing room, Ivor gave me one of his sailor suits, some pancake, and I went out, shortly, in the number, with no ice rehearsal.

All went well, except that I was the anchor as we "cracked the whip" to throw Guy into the audience, and not anticipating the snap, I went right on my butt, laughing. That didn't happen again, believe me, and I did continue to do the number. Connie Gardner, wardrobe mistress, sewed up my own, longer sailor costume for me.

After a few performances, Show Director Annie Schmidt came up and asked me if I would continue to do the number, as she needed Harris Collins, whose normal part it was, to fill in for another skater out with "Montezuma's revenge." I gladly accommodated for much of the rest of the stay... nice memories!

"My Story" by Carl Moseley

Carl Moseley, Stasa & Guy

Guy, Ivor, Todd Schoonmaker & Carl Moseley

Guy's "Sailor" Routine:
Carl, Ivor, and Todd towed Guy Longpre out onto the ice in a heavy rowboat. High jinks ensued when Stasa Longpre appeared in a sexy bathing suit. Guy called the sailors to attention, correcting Carl's stance in one ad-lib. Guy then placed a stool on the ice to stand on to match Carl's height, behind Carl, and then told Carl to turn around and face him at attention. Carl responded with a "hang dog" blank look to the audience's amusement. They broke away into a "crack the whip" with Carl as the anchor and Guy at the end, slinging Guy up into the audience! At the close, Guy would race around with a prat fall or two, then make his exit doing a cantilever under a fallen lighthouse prop.

The Pyramids of Teotihuacan

Below... Don Watson taking oxygen. Don said "Some of you HOI skaters may remember those fun days playing Arena Mexico in Mexico City... coming off the ice after performing in that altitude, you had the choice of drinking water or oxygen... covering for the ailing Arnold Shoda I chose the latter -- a safer choice!"

"My Story" by Carl Moseley

Chapter Twenty-Three

Horses and Bulls

I made three trips to Mexico City with *Holiday On Ice*, in 1965, '66, and '67. On my second trip, Tommy Collins thought it would be nice to invite, for the first time, the U.S. Ambassador to Mexico to the show. At a little reception, we presented him with a plaque commemorating *Holiday On Ice*'s many good neighbor visits to Mexico City.

All went well, and the U.S. Ambassador was so pleased that he invited our entire company to his private residence, a short distance from the city! Many went and enjoyed the food treats and drinks, etc. which he provided at his palatial home.

A couple of the chorus gals, eyeing his big beautiful pool, remarked upon it, and the Ambassador issued a kind invitation to them to come out again sometime and enjoy it. Guess what? Those gals were in his pool early the following day! They took him at his word -- that's our gypsy gals! He did not seem to mind in the least... a true ambassador!

No trip to Mexico City would be complete without a trek to Joaquin Guerra's hacienda/ranch a few miles outside of the city! Joaquin had us all there on a Monday each year, HOI providing the bus transportation. Joaquin's fine spread included, besides a large residence, a pool, tennis courts, horse stables, and a small private bull ring!

Eric Waite fell off one of the horses during one visit, and broke his foot, but somehow tough Eric toughed it out and continued to perform through the last two weeks in Mexico City.

The food, much of it authentic Mexican prepared by Joaquin's wife and other family members, was delicious and plentiful, as were the ample beverages, and a great, fun time was had by all!

The highlight of the day was a chance to actually fight a live bull! Joaquin rented a couple of "baby" bulls, for this, and any who wished could take a turn at "fighting a bull." A couple of Joaquin's men monitored on horseback for safety.

Finally, on my last trip, I got up the courage to give it a try, and "fight" a "baby" bull. "Baby" or not, those horns were not at a comfortable height, and they gave me pause, but I would have been ashamed of myself if I didn't go for it -- the last "fight" of the day!

Pictured above are Carl Moseley, Nate Walley, Joe LeMac, Antonio Huitron, Tommy Collins, & Mexico City HOI Promoter Joaquin Guerra, munching on the remains of the fried shrimp (& champagne) from the reception.

"My Story" by Carl Moseley

Carl Moseley fighting a "baby" bull

Dottie Chase Bertolino, herself, fighting a Bull in 1971

In 1957, Joaquin Guerra rescues a smiling Kay Servatious, but goes down! (Photo from Wendy Boyle's albums).

Chapter Twenty-Four
Tips from the Spin Doctor

Mexico City *Holiday On Ice* of 1965 promoter Joaquin Guerra also invited a group of us to his palatial in-town home, and, once again, Joaquin's wife and distaff family members provided a mouth-watering spread of authentic home-cooked Mexican cuisine of many flavors!

Joaquin broke out the case of Black & White Scotch that we had stashed in the Zam to bring down to him, and shared it with all. A very pleasant evening was being enjoyed by everyone in the elegant large atrium of Joaquin's home, when suddenly, around midnight, a half-dozen strolling violinists from the famous Villa Fontana restaurant emerged from behind columns to play for us, exclusively! Joaquin certainly knew how to entertain!

On a humorous note... During a bathroom visit, there, I noticed a fixture with an upturned fountain spigot, and curiously, I bent over it and turned the valve. A friend who happened to see this was soon on the floor in stitches, as I got a face-full from the bidet! Have to live to learn, I guess!

"My Story" by Carl Moseley

During HOI performances at the Arena Mexico, I would often sit by Figure Skating Director and Coach Nate Walley in rink-side seats up close to the set. I remember Ray Balmer giving Nate a thumbs up high-sign, as Ray whizzed by the front of the set, cranking up for his huge floater axel. Nate had apparently been giving Ray some tips on making it even bigger, if possible!

I observed and listened as often as possible when Nate was coaching, and I remember a lesson Ray was having with Nate on spins. Ray was holding a white handkerchief in one hand, as he pulled in his arms, so it could be seen easily if both of his arms were being kept level, as should be!

Nate, twice World Professional Champion in his Ice Capades days, could still whip off some neat steps, and on the ice with him one afternoon, I asked him to repeat one for me that he had just shown in a lesson. Nate accommodated, and I was, once again, quite impressed!

Zocalo Cathedral & Square

Carl Moseley, Tommy Collins, & Don Watson, at the reception in the residence of the U.S. Ambassador to Mexico

Some mariachis!

Carl Moseley and HOI'65 skater Linda Moseley a year before joining the show, dressed as Bat Masterson & bar-girlfriend in a "How The West Was Won" number, in a rink show.

"My Story" by Carl Moseley

Chapter Twenty-Five
One Last Visit to Chalet Suizo

Before we leave Mexico City, as the last stop on our *Holiday On Ice* of 1965 tour, I must express eternal gratitude to Juanita Percelly, who stood by me at the front of the lead bus, to and from the Chalet Suizo, on two and three show days.

My Spanish was spare, and as we got a new driver each time, Juanita was there to the rescue (as she knew the way, too, by heart) to tell him "direcho"- right, or spare me - "izquierda"- left, guiding him to the restaurant! My assignment, once there, was to do a head count near the end of each meal, in the upstairs dining room we occupied, and a last-minute check of the room and the Chalet Suizo, upon leaving, to make sure we left no gypsy behind who might have desired one more clay pot of red house wine. One had to pay for the wine, but the show paid for the food (thus my head count), which was wonderful and a real life-saver at times as a break from the spicy Mexican diet.

Our 7-year-old son, Eric, who had stayed with my parents in the Spring of 1965, joined us for the whole HOI tour the following year, and he, and Ronny LeMac, same age, took a canoe around the lake at Chapultepec Park, and disregarding official regulations, hopped off onto an island to explore it while I'm biting my nails. On a poster board by the dock to the lake, there was a large autographed photo of Canadian-born Monique Loiselle, *Holiday On Ice* unique skater, who had recently joined us!

Jimmy Crockett and Marie LaRosk (soon Crockett) became closer friends with us the first tour in '65, socializing with Linda and me for snacks and drinks after the shows in our apartment at the Golden Suites.

Finally, following a last sell-out week, including a "six-pack", our engagement in Mexico City came to an end, as indeed did *Holiday On Ice* of 1965 (U.S.A.)! All show equipment was packed up to go back to the U.S. for the use of Holiday On Ice International (U.S.A.), headed up and managed by Ed and Wilma Leary.

It was somewhat of a tradition in the days of *Holiday On Ice* of 1965 (U.S.A.), after the gags in the final show on closing night, to pour all the left-over existing booze into one batch and polish it off in a last get-together. John LaDue did not disappoint on my last night in Mexico with HOI'67, as he provided his world famous stuffed pork chops to go with the remaining hooch, in a final gathering of friends in his apartment at the Washington Square apartments.

Unless you just wanted to take the train back (we did, once), the show provided air transportation home. For us, it was a flight to Miami with a stop in Merida for customs, then on back to Tampa.

See color photo section:
Chapultepec Park & Lake, Castle, and a bull-fighting ring

Favored restaurant Chalet Suizo

"My Story" by Carl Moseley

Holiday On Ice 1966 U.S.A.

Rehearsals in Knoxville

"My Story" by Carl Moseley

Chapter Twenty-Six
A New Beginning

Holiday On Ice of 1966 (U.S.A.) was to be a watershed in HOI history, as we would be playing the big time, Madison Square Garden, New York and other major cities for the first time, taking Ice Capades' former, first ice show of the season, Fall dates in New York!

With the ownership interests of Madison Square Garden Corp., and ABC/Paramount, along with Mr. C, Morris Chalfen, the show was beefed-up majorly! The next year, I made my very first stock investment, jointly with Don Watson, in Madison Square Garden Corp. -- 100 shares at $8.00/shr. -- which made us feel like part owners of our company and the show, too, I guess.

We now had Ronnie Robertson as the star under a five-year contract, along with our regular stalwarts such as Tommy Allen Weinreich, Juanita Percelly, Ray Balmer, Alice Quessy, and other fine skaters. In addition, for the larger cities, part-tour, we had Olympic Champion Sjoukje Dijkstra and World Dance Champions Paul and Eva Roman!

The production was further enhanced by the magic-skating production of "Aladdin" by and featuring magician Harry Blackstone, Jr.,

"My Story" by Carl Moseley

son of legendary stage magician "Blackstone The Great"! To ensure productions of the highest quality, we brought over Ted Shuffle from HOI Europe to produce his Classic "24 Hours In The Day Of A Man" number starring Ronnie, and Ted's finale. Chester Hale produced his Currier & Ives winter-scene opening number, starring Tommy Allen Weinreich and Charlotte Ballauf (from Europe, too) and other numbers. To assist Chester, and work with principals, we further brought in legends Arnold Shoda and Frankie Sawers.

On top of all that, we now had, for one season, arguably the three fastest spinners in the World in one show: Ronnie Robertson, acknowledged as the fastest blur-spinner ever, and (blink and flip a coin) blur guys Tommy Allen Weinreich and Jimmy Crockett!

The 21st Edition of
HOLIDAY ON ICE
is Presented by
MORRIS CHALFEN

Executive Producer	RUTH TYSON
Executive Associate Producer	JOHN FINLEY
Music and Associate Producer	DOLORES PALLET
Staged by	CHESTER HALE

> 24 Hour Jazz Ballet and Jubilee Finale
> Produced and Staged by TED SHUFFLE

Musical Director and Arranger	BEN STABLER
Costumes Designed by	FREDDY WITTOP and MARY McKINLEY
Vocal Arrangements by	CHUCK CASSEY
Lighting Effects by	DOROTHY MORRIS

ANNE SCHMIDT	Assistant to Mr. Hale
ARNOLD SHODA	Assistant to Mr. Hale
STEPHANIE JONES	Assistant to Mr. Shuffle

HOLIDAY ON ICE is an MSG-ABC PRODUCTION. MSG-ABC PRODUCTIONS, INC. is a jointly-owned affiliate of American Broadcasting Companies, Inc. and Madison Square Garden Corporation.

MSG-ABC PRODUCTIONS, INC.
1860 Broadway, New York, N.Y. 10023

Chapter Twenty-Seven
A Perfect Place for Rehearsals

Home, in Tampa, from *Holiday On Ice* of 1965 (U.S.A.) for the month of June (almost), it was soon time to prepare for *Holiday On Ice* of 1966 (U.S.A.)! We had time to mow some grass, do a bit of home maintenance, and hit the beach once or twice, before hitting the road by car, with our seven-year-old son, Eric, and heading to Knoxville, Tennessee, for six weeks of rehearsals (including an opening week).

We had three play dates ahead of New York to polish the show - Knoxville, Nashville, and Johnstown, Pennsylvania, so rehearsals began with a bang, in earnest, to say the least! Chorus rehearsals began sharply at 8:00 a.m. Monday through Saturday, to 12:00 noon, with an hour break for lunch, during which the ice was open for principals to come in and practice. The chorus was back on again at 1:00 until 5:00 p.m.

All evening ice time was scheduled for individual principal rehearsals, lasting into the night. The show ice surface was marked off by boards on the hockey-size rink, with a row of folding chairs the whole length along one side, and the "production table" and chairs and rehearsal loudspeaker system on the opposite side.

Director Chester Hale (and wife Maureen), as well as other production staff such as Dolores Pallet sat at the table, Chester directing through

"My Story" by Carl Moseley

Annie Schmidt, on the ice. Ted Shuffle, assisted by Stephanie Jones (Stephanie Andros, now) was more of a hands-on director on the ice, himself, often with skates on.

Chester was a brilliant choreographer with a classical dance background, including "Ballet Russe de Monte Carlo" and Pavlova, Broadway, Hollywood, and Ice Capades, but he now walked with a cane and limp due to an earlier injury. Teddy was twice U.S. National Senior Men's Champion on roller skates and skated in roller Skating Vanities before HOI and Sonja Henie discovered his huge talent!

I saw Ted Shuffle late one afternoon, shortly before opening, when things were beginning to be a bit tense. Ronnie Robertson kinda' had his underwear in a bunch for some reason, making his appearance opening night seem somewhat problematic. Teddy was on the ice in khaki pants, scooting around doing lutz jumps and even a scratch spin, "just in case," I guess. I asked our new lighting director, Don Watson, if he had his skates at the ready, too!

Ronnie came around, of course, but not until after lecturing the whole watching production staff, from the ice, on dress run-through night! The Knoxville Civic Coliseum was a perfect place for rehearsals, with a full workshop and lots of space for stagehands to build new crates and work on new props and electric, etc.

The Knoxville Civic Coliseum in Knoxville, Tennessee

Executive Staff

MORRIS CHALFEN	President
EUGENE PLESHETTE	Executive Vice President
ALVIN R. GRANT	Executive Director
IRVING KLEIN	Secretary & Treasurer

Director of Advertising and Publicity .... ROBERT S. JONES
Executive Secretary to President .... MARIE SATHER
Executive Secretary New York Office .... DEDA RAPHAEL

Staff on Tour

Company Manager	TOM COLLINS
Musical Director	BEN STABLER
Stage Manager	JOE LE MAC
Asst. Company Manager	CARL MOSELEY
Performance Director	ANNE SCHMIDT
Director of Figure Skating	NATE WALLEY
Lowery-Organ	JAMES BRIMER
Captain of Girls	LUCILLE CARPENTER
Captain of Boys	ROY BUCHANAN
Chief Carpenter	AL SERIO
Chief Electrician	TED SHULTZ
Wardrobe Mistress	CONNIE GARDNER
Wardrobe Master	RON GREENQUIST
Promotion Directors	ART JOHNSON / ARTHUR SEELIG / JACK BURNETT / LARRY SADOFF
Ice Engineers	ROBERT JOHNSON / VERNE BRITTON
Lighting Director	DON WATSON
Concession Manager	JOE EASTEN
Program Sales	GERALD COLLINS

Holiday On Ice
FALL ITINERARY

				Days
Knoxville, Tenn.	Rehearsals	Thur. June 30 - Sun. Aug. 7	39
Knoxville, Tenn.	Civic Coliseum	Mon. Aug. 8 - Sun. Aug. 14	7
Nashville, Tenn.	Municipal Auditorium	Tues. Aug. 16 - Sun. Aug. 21	6
Johnstown, Pa.	Cambria County War Memorial	Tues. Aug. 23 - Sun. Aug. 28	6
New York, N. Y.	Madison Square Garden	Wed. Aug. 31 - Sun. Sept. 18	19

Inside the Knoxville Civic Coliseum

"My Story" by Carl Moseley

Chapter Twenty-Eight

Sloopy, Hang On!

Rehearsals for *Holiday On Ice* of 1966 (U.S.A.) began in earnest in Knoxville, as there were only two more dates after opening in Knoxville, before the biggie, New York City and Madison Square Garden -- *Holiday On Ice*'s first visit there, coming up!

Our HOI show office at the Knoxville Civic Coliseum was in an empty store-front above the lobby, and the HOI production office next door, behind a thin partition, was used for meetings by the production staff: Producer Ruth Tyson ("Mrs. T"), Associate Producer John Finley, Music Producer Dolores Pallet, Director/Choreographers Chester Hale and Ted Shuffle, Ted's assistant Stephanie Jones (Stephanie Andros, now), and Music Director, Arranger, Composer, and Conductor Ben Stabler.

As the partition was thin, we could often hear snippets of conversations, and as things got closer to the opening wire, more rather heated discussions going on! John Finley, an individual, if ever there was one, took Don Watson and I along on a visit to the first K-Mart I had ever seen, where John bought a pair of blue khaki pants, which he said he was going to wear every day until we opened (as a nerve-calmer, I surmised).

Through the same partition, a couple of years later, for the "Paris á Nuit" Go Go number of HOI'68, we could hear Ted Shuffle recording the prologue with a hand-held mike: "Paris remembered ... It was Paris, and we were so much in love...etc." and then Teddy singing "Hang on, Sloopy, Sloopy Hang On!" Yep, that was Ted on the performance tape voice-over!

Into our show office, to my amazement and awe, walked Don Watson, about whom I had heard so much from my skating buddy, Roger Gross. Roger who used to rave about Don, another arena "ghost", saying that he often practiced so hard in cold, darkened arenas that the sweat on his back froze through his t-shirt!

In any case, I relayed this to Don on the spot, who, at the time must have thought I was nuts! Don Watson was between employments, having just finished a year-long run at the Chicago Hilton, and HOI Manager Tommy Collins seized the opportunity to add Don to our show staff as our new Lighting Director and also as Production Assistant to John Finley.

Don Watson and I became fast friends ("skating buddies") and are to this day, having shared many adventures on the following three tours of Holiday On Ice (U.S.A.)

See color photo section: Photos of the Andrew Johnson Hotel in Knoxville, where many of us stayed in those days of old!

My first little (innocent) 14-year-old girlfriend, Joyce Trainor.

"My Story" by Carl Moseley

Carl Moseley and Joyce Trainor. Carl reports: "Joyce and her mother, to my surprise, showed up in Knoxville during our opening of HOI'68, twenty years later!"

Chapter Twenty-Nine
A Special Video Collection

That first year in Knoxville, for rehearsals and opening of *Holiday On Ice* of 1966 (U.S.A.), many of us from the show stayed in a nice but rather small apartment motel with a central pool. In later years, however, it was to be at "the AJ," the Andrew Johnson Hotel, with most everyone else in the show. Chester Hale and his wife, Maureen were there, too, and Chester swam laps in the pool for exercise, as he had an earlier leg injury which prevented him other exercise. Our son Eric was often in the pool at the same time, and Chester took a liking to him, with playful water fights, etc.!

As we had driven to Knoxville and had room in the car, I brought along my 8 mm movie projector and began showing my collection of ice show numbers. One night, most of the HOI gang crammed into our motel room to watch them and to perhaps see themselves on film for the first time, such as Ray Balmer, Alice Quessy, and Tommy Allen Weinreich, filmed in *Holiday On Ice* of 1963 (U.S.A.).

Arnold Shoda was pretty amazed at seeing himself in the 50's at the Chicago Hilton (Sherman), and Joan Hyldoft, too, in the film which I had copied, on loan, from Joan!

"My Story" by Carl Moseley

My paperwork load, in spite of no performance reports until actual opening, was multiplied in Knoxville, as invoices for all materials for work on props, electric, new crate construction at the shop in the building, etc. crossed my desk, and had to be verified by me with the various department heads, and then paid! Believe me, there were plenty of nails, screws, lumber, casters, and wire involved!

Knoxville Scenic Studios provided the new dressings for the set and large props, and was paid ahead of time for same, by our Cleveland office. The large payroll, too, was done from scratch by me, instead of in Cleveland, until we got rolling on the road -- it was no picnic each week! Not to complain... you take the good with the bad. I returned to our building office to catch up, often in the evenings, and was able to observe some principal rehearsals, including watching Ted Shuffle coaching and rehearsing Ronnie Robertson in Ted's classic "24 Hours In The Life Of A Man" number!

After that, the ice was free, and, as I had the run of the building, knew where to turn the lights on and off, etc. I often put my skates on and blew off steam for a while on almost exclusive ice that was pleasingly soft, and in a shirt-sleeve temperature building!

See color photo section:
HOI'66 Program Cover and Ray Ballmer number

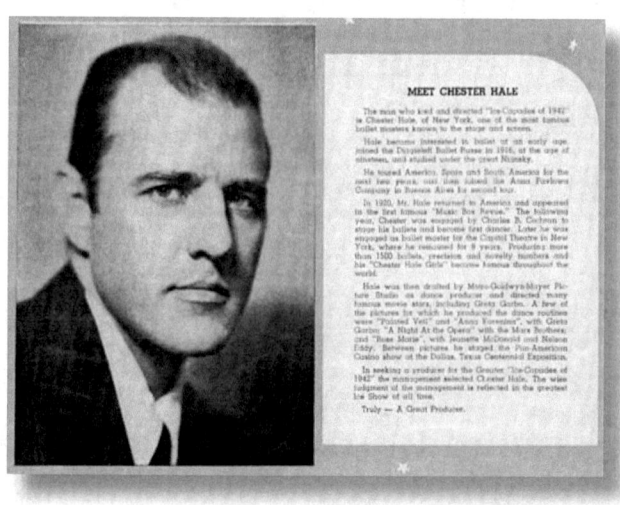

Chester Hale conducting a ballet class at his Carnegie Hall Studio

*Alice Quessy &
Ray Ballmer*

"My Story" by Carl Moseley

Chapter Thirty
That's the Way You Do It!

During the rehearsal of a military precision number, my son Eric came marching down, to the music, right in front of Chester and the production table, breaking up the kids and prompting Chester to say, laughingly: "That's the way you do it!" It was probably high time for bit of levity, anyway!

John Finley! Now there was an interesting fellow! John, HOI Associate Producer (but probably de facto Producer, as Producer Ruth Tyson was getting on a bit), headed up the HOI production office in New York, right on Broadway.

I visited the NY office once to view the miniature set mock-ups andcostume sketches, etc. John Finley, was a bit of a type A, I would venture to say, at least as rehearsals progressed (or didn't progress). As I mentioned earlier, he swore to wear a blue pair of Kmart pants every day until opening night - maybe as good luck omen?

Anyway, Don Watson was John Finley's production assistant during rehearsals in Knoxville, but as I had my car there, John had me drive him about 20 miles or so along the refreshing Tennessee River to a place that was restoring a sports car for John. I got to know John a bit better, and he was actually a very nice guy. John Finley's wife was a hot looking gal with red-orange hair, someone hard to forget.

One year, in Mexico City, Tommy Collins was talking to John on expensive long distance, in New York, for an hour or so, supposedly on show business, but actually yacking back and forth with John about all the latest love-life, intrigue, and gossip transpiring! John had been with *Holiday On Ice* for a long time, paying his dues, to finally reach his production executive position When U.S. *Holiday On Ice* was merged with Ice Follies in 1979, and HOI became a clone of Ice Follies in subsequent years, there was no longer a need for a separate *Holiday On Ice* production office and staff, so John moved on to other pursuits!

The last time I saw John was in the 70's when John, then company manager for the "Lippizaner Stallions" horse show, invited Alice Quessy to the show in Tampa, and Alice included Linda Moseley and me for front row seats and a nice greeting and tour by John!

At lunch time, Don Watson and I often sat at the vaulted but empty production table, munching on sandwiches kept in the building fridge and perusing the progress (usually) of the various principals as they practiced.

John Finley

Chester Hale

"My Story" by Carl Moseley

An international favorite, Tommy Allen, thrills Holiday on Ice audiences with his fantastic skating skill.

Tommy Allen Weinreich, gloriously landing his big open axel, in Holiday On Ice of 1966. I remember watching Tommy Allen Weinreich doing, over and over, right up front, his big, open, floating axel, perfecting the gorgeous landing position you can see in the picture!

Chapter Thirty-One
Sets & Rigs & the AJ

The ice for rehearsals in Knoxville was marked off to show size by boards, with a long row of folding chairs on one side for chorus members, awaiting in practice clothes and/or robes, for their calls to the ice, and the production table and sound system on the other. The normal backstage ice, where the set was to be hung, was open for anyone to warm up or stretch their legs a bit, and the front end of the ice had been extended beyond show size to include a patch behind a black curtain for ancillary work on steps, etc.

After Eric Waite's foot injury the following year in Mexico City, Eric could be found daily behind that black curtain, going round and round, in a figure-eight pattern, somewhat in pain, working it out to prove wrong doctors who told Eric it was time to hang up his skates.

We got a new, supposedly lighter-weight aluminum set frame in Knoxville, and Tommy Collins had Stage Manager Joe LeMac and me weigh it, piece by piece, on a huge industrial scale, to be sure. We didn't want to pull any building ceiling beams down that weren't strong enough!

"My Story" by Carl Moseley

As things progressed, and more and more props, etc. were brought in for this huge edition of HOI. Harry Blackstone's magical apparatus for the "Aladdin" number was large and complicated things, especially as Harry's "levitation" rig was delicate and time-consuming, to be set up just right, anchored in the ice under the set... so Alice Quessy would unfailingly be levitated by Harry!

Tommy Collins decided that we would do a "practice" move-out, a week before opening, to be sure we could get everything into our nineteen HOI "wagons". Well, with stagehands, we tackled it, and the sun was just rising as we closed the last wagon, out in back of the Civic Coliseum! Normally the show had to be fully packed into the train by about 1:00 a.m. after a Sunday last show ending at 8:00 p.m., so Tommy said: "Some of this stuff has got to go!" Some of it did, and we were actually able to pack it up closing night in Knoxville -- more about that, later, and my adventures on the move-out and move-in "baggage car crew," later!

Toward the end of the first week of rehearsals in Knoxville, we had a big rehearsal opening party at the AJ (Andrew Johnson Hotel), to welcome new members and for all to get acquainted or re-acquainted, whichever the case... and they did! It was a blast, and among the feeling-good crowd emerged two super-looking gals, Diane Pott (Diane Robinson, now) and Cathy Johnson, apparently "feeling good" as they announced to me, side-by-side, that they were the new "party girls" (to put it kindly) of the show!

Somewhat taken aback, and feeling pretty good myself, I struggled to contain my reaction (might not have, completely) to this declaration, by two fine gals who were just having fun after a strenuous rehearsal week, and who became good friends with me, and all, for a long time!

*See color photo section:
Ray Balmer & Alice Quessy in
Harry Blackstone, Jr.'s "Aladdin"
production*

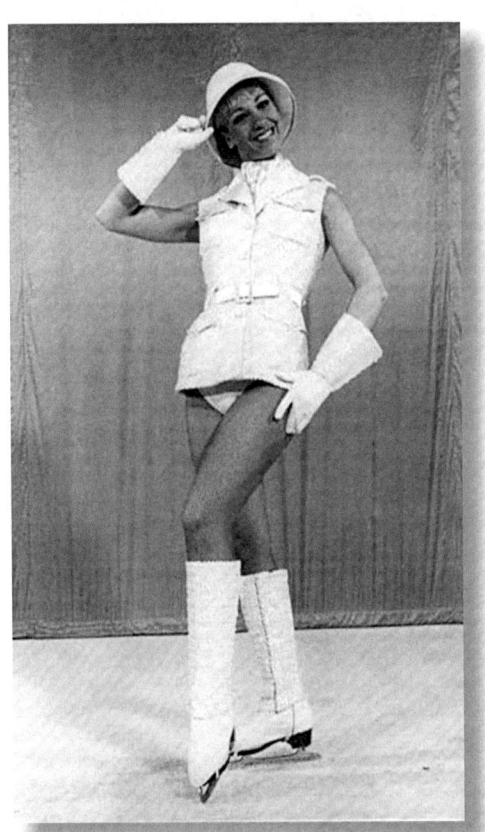

Diane Pott

Mystical Illusions and Effects
created by
America's Foremost Magician
HARRY BLACKSTONE, Jr.

Chapter Thirty-Two

Mrs T

Picking up rehearsals in Knoxville, Tennessee, here's a little bit about *Holiday On Ice* Producer Ruth Tyson ("Mrs. T"), who was a gentle, kind, but firm lady, and most of all -- a lady!

Mrs. T had been a hoofer on the stage in her early years and knew show business backwards and forwards! She was married to George Tyson, general manager of Ice Capades, for John H. Harris, in earlier times, and George and Mrs. T became producers of *Holiday On Ice* for Morris Chalfen, later. George had passed several years before, but back in 1948, when my dad was the local promoter for *Holiday On Ice* in Tampa, he took George Tyson and Mrs. T to the famous Spanish restaurant in "Ybor City," the Columbia Restaurant, which featured Spanish dancers in the floor show and a strolling violinist, as well!

My dad also showed them Florida west coast beach property near his, before George decided to buy in Coral Gables near Miami, and also rehearse HOI there, at the Coral Gables Coliseum. Mrs. T was always receptive to any talented skater who was motivated and willing to work hard, titled or not, to move up from the chorus, and she was helpful to many! Jimmy Crockett told me that his airline ticket was cut, back to California from Knoxville, as Jimmy didn't seem to fit the mold as a chorus skater as much as others in the final selections, but that Mrs. T caught a glimpse of Jimmy doing his stuff in practice and put a hold on it, telling Jimmy that we, HOI, may have a little something for you after all!

Joel Parks, another very talented skater, joined us in the chorus in Knoxville for HOI'66, and Joel had as his goal, a move upward to featured status. He did, becoming a principal in *Holiday On Ice* Europe, starring in Ted Shuffle's "Counterpoint" number and also in the Vienna Eisrevue! I encouraged Joel Parks in his pursuits, as did Jimmy Crockett.

About a week before opening in Knoxville, we were all surprised and somewhat stunned when Ronnie Robertson showed up at lunchtime principal practice ice for the first time. Ronnie had been working with Ted Shuffle many evenings, exclusively, on his solo in Ted's "24 Hours In The Life Of A Man" production, some of which rehearsals I had been privy to watch. He and proceeded to do a run-through with music, and no faking, of his four-minute plus "24 Hour" solo!

We were all taken aback, as Ronnie flew around the ice, clearing house and cleaning up, but also giving us a puff-puff look, with a grin, as he made the last go-round in this great number! You can watch the video, I filmed, of Ronnie:
https://www.youtube.com/watch?v=YOTrKOYIapc

Ruth Tyson

See color photo section:
Chorus Gals

"My Story" by Carl Moseley

*Ronnie Robertson as in HOI'66
(above and below)*

Chapter Thirty-Three

The Houn' Dog & A Latin Lover

As I mentioned earlier, Joel Chandler Parks was among the new talented hopefuls to join us in rehearsals in Knoxville. Promising pair skaters Ron Basten and Chickie Berlin, whom we had signed in Miami Beach the Spring before, came in, too, and *Holiday On Ice* regulars, Gene Theslof (Jr.), and his wife Sara were back again and were warming up some nice adagio moves for future consideration by the powers that be.

One of those adagio moves was producer Ruth Tyson's "baby" -- the Houn' Dawg skin number, featuring Alfredo Mendoza, front and John Ladue, rear. Mrs.T conducted the rehearsals for Alfredo and John in this number personally and exclusively! Both John and Alfredo were multi-talented skaters, filling many various rolls in HOI.

Alfredo's brothers were cliff divers in Acapulco (Alfie did it too, I hear), and he was in the Guinness Book of World Records as the only one to win, at the time, two World Water Ski Championships. He was sorta' known as "The Latin Lover," at least by us on the office staff, and with good reason!

"My Story" by Carl Moseley

Alfredo, having been once married to Jinx Clark, had an uncanny sense of homing in on top gal stars of the show. Alfie's girlfriend of the day, in '65-'66, was Brenda Zellman, who skated with Alfredo in the comedy/adagio/trio spoof. She also understudied Janie Morris, Alfredo's "straight" adagio partner, in Alfredo and Janie's fine, starring adagio roles!

Brenda woke up most residents of the AJ (Andrew Johnson Hotel) late one evening, pounding on Alfredo's door, accusing him of having an unnamed paramour within, bringing on the hotel house security!

The coffee stand during rehearsals in Knoxville, operated by Lucy Carpenter, offered donuts, danishes, etc. It was close to the door, on the chorus side of the ice, and was a gathering place in the mornings. Alfredo showed up there one morning, much earlier than necessary for him, and perused, as we all did, I guess, the new "merchandise! (attributable to the roughly 30% turnover in lovely chorus gals).

As weeks rolled on, and we got closer to the wire of opening night, Annie conducted some practice costume changes, timing the kids to make sure they could get back to the dressing rooms, change to a new costume, and return to the backstage ice within the time allotted between numbers. Then, in the last week before opening night, we had a series of "run-throughs" of the whole show, each one getting closer to the real thing.

First, with costumes, then next with costumes and performance lights, and finally one run-through before dress rehearsal, with an invited full-house audience, with costumes, lights, and live music! The first time the kids heard Benny Stabler and his show orchestra perform this heretofore recorded music, just before opening, it came as an unfamiliar shock to many, to say the least. All persevered, and Benny's music soon became familiar and most reassuring to all.

During the last run-though, Ronnie Robertson, who had been in a mood of a sort, stopped the show and came up to the front seats where all the production staff were sitting (me, too), and proceeded to lecture all of us about the conduct of the proceedings, thus far! Taken like water off a duck's back, and Ronnie, having blown off steam, he was now more relaxed, things soon fell into place, and all went well.

The Houn' Dog Number with Alfred Mendoza & John Ladue, and Janie Morris and, in earlier times, Barbara Oshust

ALFREDO MENDOZA . . .
This handsome fellow from south of the border was the world's champion water skier when he saw a performance of "Holiday on Ice" at Tampa, Fla. and decided to become a skater. He bought skates, carried them with him all over the world, practicing whenever he got a chance. He would travel hundreds of miles to get to an ice rink. Finally he sought an audition with "Holiday" and was accepted as a chorus skater. Then he had the opportunity to train, and train he did, morning, noon and after the show. His efforts paid off and Alfredo is now rated one of the world's fine adagio skaters.

See color photo section:
Joel Chandler Parks, later in Europe, with Linda Adams Garl, & Ronnie Robertson

Chapter Thirty-Four

Levitation & Laughter

Dress rehearsal survived (barely), *Holiday On Ice* of 1966 (U.S.A.) was finally a reality, as we opened in Knoxville for a week run. The show was well received in Knoxville, as usual, with so many local folks having been involved in the building of the show.

There was a traditional opening night, dressy, dinner party for all after the show at the Andrew Johnson Hotel. Everything was most elegant, and magician Harry Blackstone, Jr. entertained, impromptu, as he casually walked up to a table full of folks and proceeded to grasp one fellow's shirt by the collar and pull the shirt right off his back without removing his coat, amazing all at the table!

Harry Blackstone, Jr. had successfully "levitated" Alice Quessy during the show, and our seven-year-old son Eric went up to Harry and asked him to make him float a bit, too. Harry said to Eric: "O.K. lift up your left leg," which Eric did, and then Harry said "Now, lift up your right leg," to which Eric said, "I can't do that." Harry then responded: "Well, if you can't do that, how do you expect me to make you float?" to the laughter of all!

Another casual, but lively and well-needed party was thrown by Frankie Sawers at a house in Knoxville where Frankie was staying about mid-way through rehearsals, and was a well-received tension reliever, to say the least, at that point!

Harry Blackstone Jr.'s wife, Joyce Wells, a very nice gal, had skated in *Holiday On Ice* in earlier days, and joined us once more in the show, for the duration of Harry's involvement. During our New York City engagement a few weeks later, Harry and Joyce invited our son Eric to stay with them a couple days in their posh apartment, rented for our three-week stay in New York!

During our performance week in Knoxville, the show was further polished and tightened up by Annie Schmidt, Chester Hale, Ted Shuffle, and assisting production folks, Stephanie Jones (Andros), Frankie Sawers, and Arnold Shoda, who stuck close until after we opened in New York.

Ronnie Robertson, as I filmed him in his "Gypsy" solo: https://www.youtube.com/watch?v=Cq_zl_J_0EE :

Ray Balmer, Tommy Allen Weinreich, Juanita Percelly, and others, in the "Musical Comedy Americana" number.
See color photo section for more!

COLOR PHOTO SECTION

Holiday On Ice 1966 U.S.A.

Moving On to the Big Apple

"My Story" by Carl Moseley

3A   Cover of program for Holiday On Ice 1965 (U.S.A.)

 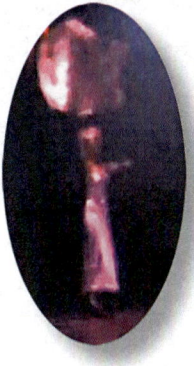

4A & 4B
Here's Linda
Moseley in the
HOI'65 opening
"Feather" number

"My Story" by Carl Moseley

5A Jackie Gleason's Auditorium in Miami Beach -- There was a huge birthday cake made of flowers, in front, when the author was there.

7A Holiday On Ice "hip-swinging, gum-chewing chorines" of the day (actually very fine ensemble skaters), Terry Cramer Kessler King & Olivia Gardner-Hawley

12A HOI'65 -- *our lovely, lovely, show gals, all fondly remembered!*

"My Story" by Carl Moseley

13A   Stars of Holiday On Ice 1965

25B Pictured above is Chapultepec Park & Lake, more commonly called the "Bosque de Chapultepec" (Chapultepec Forest) in Mexico City

25C Bull-fighting ring in Mexico

25D Chapultepec Castle

"My Story" by Carl Moseley

25E Arena in Mexico

28C & 28D
Photos of the Andrew Johnson Hotel in Knoxville, where many of us stayed in those days of old!

"My Story" by Carl Moseley

30A & 30B
HOI'66
Program cover featuring Principals and Ray Ballmer's Number

31C & 31D Ray Balmer & Alice Quessy in Harry Blackstone, Jr.'s "Aladdin" production

"My Story" by Carl Moseley

32B HOI'66 Chorus Gals

32C & 32D
Joel Chandler Parks, later in Europe, with Linda Adams Garl (left)

Ronnie Robertson (below)

34B & 34C
Ray Balmer, Tommy Allen Weinreich, Juanita Percelly, and others, in "Musical Comedy Americana" (above)

The guys & gals in Ronnie Robertson's "Gypsy" number (left)

"My Story" by Carl Moseley

34D
Bill Dyer's caricature cartoon in the Knoxville News-Sentinel depicting Holiday On Ice rehearsals, c. 1966

35C & 35D
Jimmy Crockett, John Ladue, Ronny LeMac, & Sandy Wirwill, in the "kiddy" number, HOI'66, "Picnic At The Kiddy Zoo" (above & below)

"My Story" by Carl Moseley

36D
HOI'66 program photos, including Karl Kossmayer's mules

37A & 37B
HOI'66 Jubilee Finale

"My Story" by Carl Moseley

37C
An example of the big skirts the ladies had to learn to skate in for Holiday On Ice productions... don't trip!

38C
Johnstown Flood

39D
Advertisement for Holiday On Ice and the new Madison Square Garden

"My Story" by Carl Moseley

40A   HOI'66 Program Page

40B   HOI '66 Program photo

43B
Paul & Eva Roman
HOI'66

44B
Radio City Music Hall

"My Story" by Carl Moseley

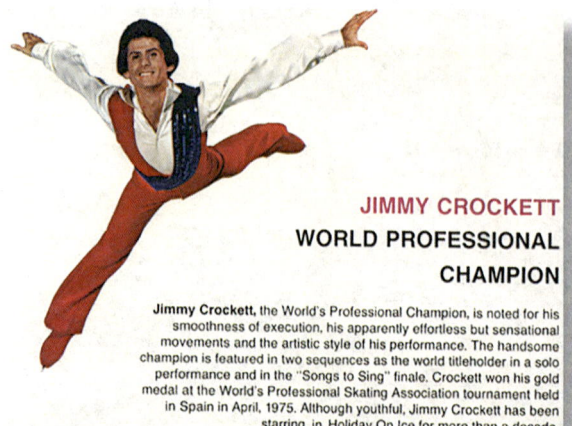

45A
Jimmy Crockett

47A & 47B
*Ronnie Robertson &
Flying high for the Ladies*

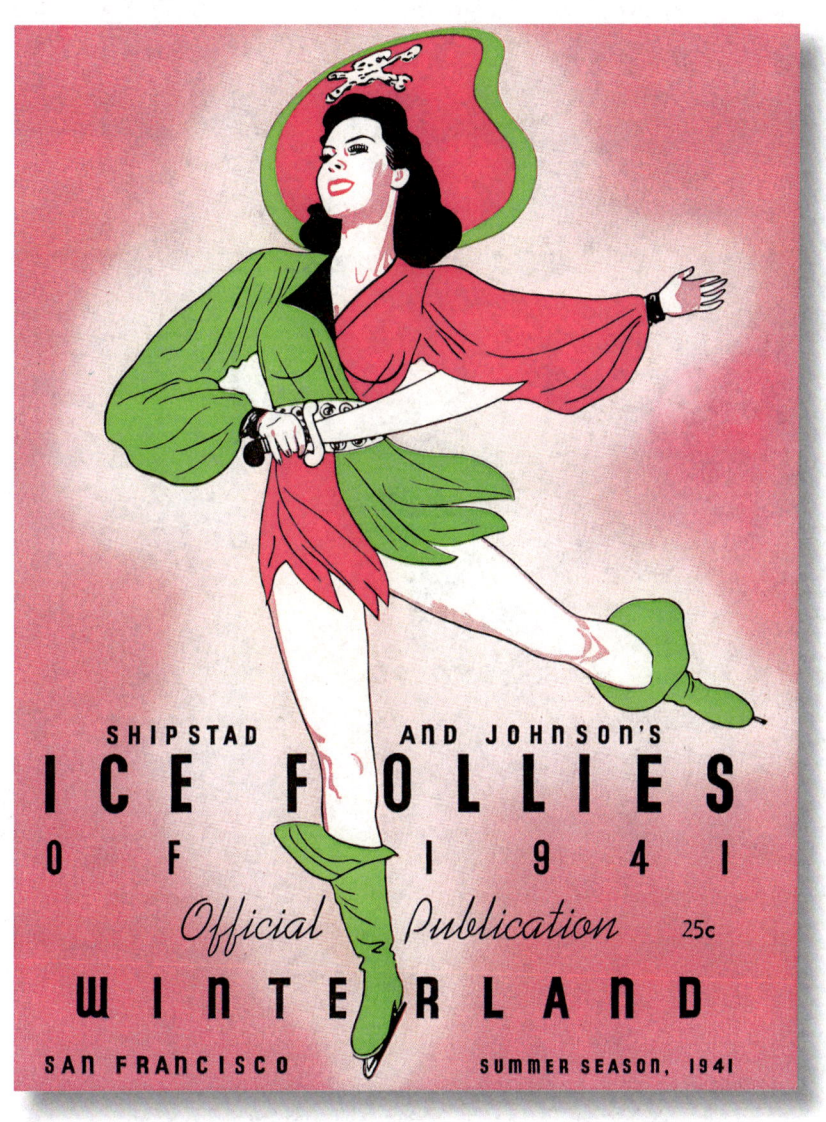

48B
Ice Follies 1941 at the Winterland

"My Story" by Carl Moseley

48D
Ronnie Robertson

49A
Maple Leaf Gardens

49D
Ed Sullivan Show & Ronnie Robertson

50B
Reno, Nevada, The Biggest Little City in the World.

"My Story" by Carl Moseley

52A, 52B & 52C:
The Pan-Pacific
Auditorium (above)

Disneyland Castle (right)
and

the Hollywood Farmer's
Market (below)

53C & 53D
The Barbary Coast (above) & The Empire Builder Train (right)

54C
Yvonne Conley & Sandy Wirwill at the Hollywood Opener

54D
Ray Balmer

"My Story" by Carl Moseley

54E The Davis Islands Coliseum (Tampa, Florida)

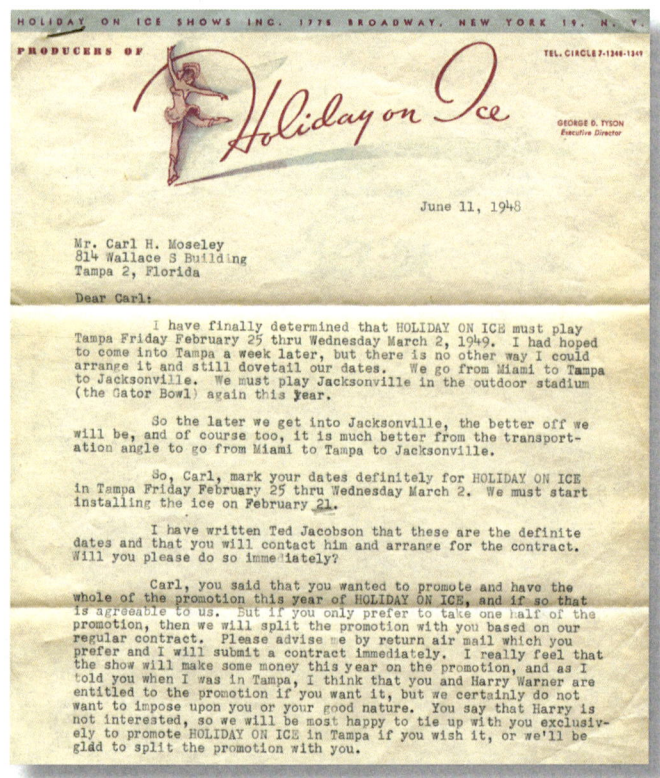

54F Letter to the author's dad regarding promotion proposal (1948)

Feb. 9th 1966
6020 Roselawn
Dayton, Ohio
45430

Dear ???
    I'm not quite sure to whom I should address this letter but I shan't let that stop me.
    My husband and I had front row seats for the show last night and I felt a thank you was in order.
    I laughed until I cried, clapped until my hands burned, and admired you all until we left. The whole show was fabulous.
    My son, who is 2, has a favorite... a certain penguin who left the ice and gave him a piece of candy.
    The next time you get tired and a little bored or maybe homesick, remember this... for a few minutes you give people a chance to live in a world full of very beautiful things where laughter and joy preceedes all else, and in a world filled with hate, anger, and strife, what greater gift can one man give another than a little happiness.

A true fan,

Judy Jones

6020 Roselawn Dr.
Dayton, Ohio
    45430

P.S. I hope all of you can read this letter for I feel you deserve more praise that a hand clap.

54G
This letter was sent to us, Holiday On Ice of 1966, while playing Dayton, Ohio, and posted on our back-stage call board, but it is for every one of you show skaters, and all who ever did a three-show Saturday, or maybe a "six-pack" week-end, and wondered if it was worth it!

"My Story" by Carl Moseley

54H
The Davis Islands Coliseum in Tampa, Florida (above)

59B & 59C
The Indian Rocks Beach cottage now, transformed into the Historical Museum

62A & 62B *The Philadelphia Skating Club & Humane Society*

62C *A plate of spaghetti and meatballs from The Roma*

"My Story" by Carl Moseley

63D
Lucy Lee Flippen, Holiday On Ice skater

63B
Dorian Shields Valles

64C
Ice Follies program page featuring Barbara Myers

```
ENGAGEMENT INFORMATION SHEET              COPIES:
   (AVOID QUESTIONS BY READING CAREFULLY)      SHOW MANAGER
                                               BULLETIN BOARD
                                               STAGE MANAGER
                                               ALL DEPT. HEADS
                                               ADVANCE MAN
                                               OFFICE FILE

NEXT ENGAGEMENT: MEXICO CITY
PLAYDATES: FRI. MAY 5TH THRU SUN. JUNE 4TH, 1967
PERFORMANCE TIMES: NIGHTLY AT: SEE SPECIAL NOTICE  EXCEPT:
MATINEE TIMES:

CHECK IN OPENING NIGHT: 4:00 PM
NAME OF BUILDING: ARENA MEXICO
BUS TO AND FROM BUILDING... YES — NO
SHOW OFFICE LOCATED IN: MONTE CASSINO HOTEL  PHONE NUMBER: 25-15-80
MANAGER LIVING AT:           "    "    "
BANK: SEE NOTICE
DOCTOR:           "    "
TRUNKS DOWNSTAIRS AT LOADING DOCK:
STAGEHAND CALL AT BUILDING: 6:00 AM FRI. MAY 5TH
ORCHESTRA REHEARSAL: 10:00 AM FRI. MAY 5TH
WHERE:
CALL TO UNLOAD WAGONS: MEET AT MONTE CASSINO HOTEL AT 9:00 AM THURS. MAY 4TH


             TRAIN SCHEDULE FOR SHOW PERSONNEL
NAME OF STATION: UNION TERMINAL
COACH, PULLMAN AND/OR BUS TRIP:
DINER ON TRAIN... YES — NO
PULLMANS READY FOR OCCUPANCY AT: 12:01 AM WED. MAY 3RD   NUEVO LAREDO TO MEXICO CITY
OCCUPY PULLMANS UNTIL: ARRIVAL IN MEXICO CITY
CHECK IN AT DEPOT: 3:00 AM
REMARKS: THE STATION IN SAN ANTONIO HAS ONLY A SNACK BAR...HOWEVER THERE IS A
         RESTAURANT ONE BLOCK AWAY.

                                              RAILROAD & TRAIN NUMBER
LV: THIS CITY    3:30 AM WED. MAY 3        SANTA FE EXTRA
AR:              SAN ANTONIO 12:00 NOON
LV:                "      "   1:45 PM      MP # 1
AR:              LAREDO        5:20 PM
LV:              NUEVO LAREDO  6:00 PM     NRR EXTRA
AR:
LV:
AR: NEXT ENGAGEMENT  5:00 PM THURS. MAY 4TH
```

Holiday On Ice 1967
Engagement Information Sheet

"My Story" by Carl Moseley

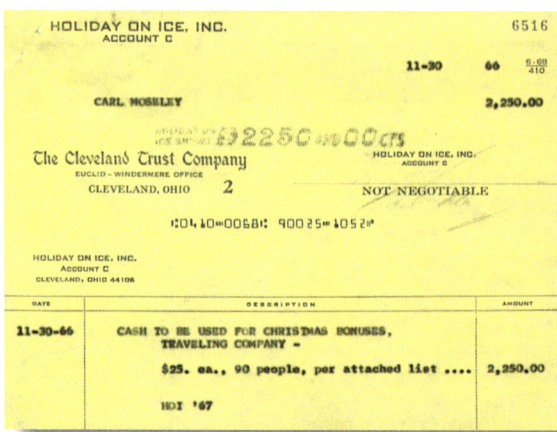

Holiday On Ice 1967 Check for cash to be used in gift cards for Christmas bonuses; Below, bonus list -- to receive $25.00 cash each!

CHRISTMAS BONUSES   HOI '67
$ 25. EA:

TOM COLLINS
GERALD COLLINS
CARL MOSELEY
DON WATSON
ANNE SCHMIDT

JAMES COATNEY
FRANK J. FOSTER
JOE LEMAC
DONALD NASHLEANAS
JERRY NASHLEANAS
MERRILL RICHARDSON
AL SERIO
TED SHULTZ
R. H. THORNHILL
JAMES THURMAN
MARVIN WHITE
JOE WILLIAMS

CHARLOTTE BALLAUF
RAY BALMER
PETRA BURKA
KARL KOSSMAYER
JOHN LADUE
ALICE QUESSY
RONNIE LEMAC
GUY LONGPRE
PEGGY McCUTCHEON
JANE McCUTCHEON
ALFREDO MENDOZA
JANE MORRIS
JUANITA PERCELLY
RONNIE ROBERTSON
IVOR ROBSON
MARTY RYAN
LOU SASCHE
ERIC WAITE
TOMMY ALLEN
SANDY WIRWILL

LINDA BALTZLEY
KAREN CARPENTER
PAT CLOHESSY
ROSEMARIE COATNEY
YVONNE CONLEY

NATE WALLEY
JOE EASTON
FRANK MICALE

NANCY DeHAYS
ALIX EBSEN
SHIRLEY BDGCOMB
DIXIE GINN
GAIL GROS
CLAUDETTE KENALTY
KATHY JOHNSON
SUZANNE LABAK
STASA LONGPRE
ANDREA MARTIN
ROXANNE MAXCY
EILENE MEREDITH
JOELLA MILAN
LINDA MOSELEY
KUNIKO NAKAJIMA
DIANE POTT
HELLA RATHJE
THELMA RICKETT
CINDY SACHSE
JUDY SCHNUUR
BARBARA SCHOONMAKER
LUCILLE CARPENTER
BARBARA SMITH
SARA THESLOF
ADRI VERZAAL
JUDY WALIN
IRMA WALSER
BRENDA ZELLMAN

RON BASTEN
ROGER BATHURST
GORDON BETSILL
CHRIS BRUYNIUS
ROY BUCHANAN
MIKE BURNS
HARRIS COLLINS
LUCIEN LA CROIX
LONNIE MC CALL
TODD SCHOONMAKER
BIL STOSIC
GENE THESLOF
CHARLES VIDONNE

JAMES BRIMER
JAMES PITTMAN
BEN STABLER
DAVE WILSON

TOTAL: 90 @ $25. ... **$2,250.00**

CASH IN LIEU OF RAIL TRANSPORTATION, MEXICO CITY, SAN ANTONIO ....

	Name		Destination			Total
	ALL FOREIGNERS (& APRIL ADAMS)		New York	21.00 &	69.86	$ 90.86
	LUCILLE CARPENTER		MIAMI	"	49.07	70.07
	ROSEMARIE COATNEY		KNOXVILLE	"	36.43	57.43
	NANCY DE HAYS		DAYTON	"	45.67	66.67
	DIXIE GINN		MEMPHIS	"	25.43	46.43
	KATHY JOHNSON		MIAMI	"	49.07	70.07
	STASA LONGPRE		SHERBROOKE	"	74.37	95.37
	CLAUDETTE KENALTY		MONTREAL	"	70.32	91.32
	GUY LONGPRE		SHERBROOKE	"	74.37	95.37
	ANDREA MARTIN		DAYTON	45.67	45.67	66.67
	EILENE MEREDITH		ST. PETERSBURG	"	47.57	68.57
	BARBARA SMITH		EVANSTON, ILL.	"	42.25	63.25
	VIVIAN SOMMERS		SAN FRANCISCO	"	59.06	80.06
	SARA THESLOF		EVANSVILLE	"	34.59	55.59
	GENE THESLOF		"	"	"	"
	ROGER BATHURST		INDIANA, PA.	"	55.46	76.46
	RON BASTEN		NEW FRANKEN, WISC.	"	48.26	69.26
	GORDON BETSILL		ATLANTA	"	34.86	55.86
	MIKE BURNS		NORMAL, ILL.	"	39.20	60.20
	HARRIS COLLINS		MINNEAPOLIS	"	45.65	66.65
	WILLIAM DUKE		ATLANTA	"	34.86	55.86
	LUCIEN LA CROIX		MANVILLE, R.I.	"	79.12	100.12
	JOEL PARKS		MIAMI	"	49.07	70.07
	JANE McCUTCHEON		BELLVILLE, CANADA	"	65.53	86.53
	PEGGY McCUTCHEON		" "	"	"	"
	SANDY WIRWILL		DETROIT	"	49.30	70.30
	ALICE QUESSY		CLEARWATER	"	44.47	65.47
	RONNIE LEMAC		"	"	"	"
	JOHN LADUE		PLATTSBURG, N.Y.	"	76.72	97.72
	PETRA BURKA		TORONTO	"	57.91	78.91
CREW:	DON NASHLEANAS	(1st)	SIOUX CITY	"	68.83	89.83
	JERRY NASHLEANAS	"	" "	"	"	"
	JOE LEMAC	"	CLEARWATER	"	61.47	82.47
	FRANK FOSTER	"	NEW YORK	"	83.96	104.96
	AL SERIO	"	" "	"	"	"
	TED SHULTZ	"	SUNBURY, PA.	"	72.91	93.91
	MARVIN WHITE	"	ASHLAND, KY.	"	64.73	85.73
	JOEL WILLIAMS	"	SAN FRANCISCO	"	74.99	95.99
MUSIC.	JAMES BRIMER	(Air)	KNOXVILLE	/		99.64
	DAVE WILSON	"	"			"
	JAMES PITTMAN	"	TAMPA			89.88
STAFF	GERALD COLLINS	(1st)	MINNEAPOLIS	(Air "to San Antonio)		45.65
	CARL MOSELEY	"	TAMPA	21.00	61.47	82.47
	DON WATSON		FT. WORTH	"	11.87	32.87
	JAMES COATNEY		KNOXVILLE	"	36.43	57.43
	JOE EASTON		CHICAGO	"	42.25	63.25
	MERRILL RICHARDSON		Air Ticket to Miami			

"Cash in lieu of rail transportation" from Mexico City. The train trip was fun the first time, but taking the trip back from Mexico City was very monotonous, and required many train changes in some cases, so some opted to fly home instead. Some also took a vacation in Acapulco or Merida to relax a bit before going home.

"My Story" by Carl Moseley

```
                        HOLIDAY ON ICE OF 1966

OPENING NUMBER: - RHYTHM, PRECISION AND FUN

MUSIC AND TIMING:   (Overture to come to a false finish and segue)

Into "In Old New York" - (This to cut off after 28th bar of chorus to allow for
business of camera flash and picture coming to life.  The first 28 bars in B.O.
lights up on picture last 4 bars.                                         :31
                              SEGUE

Skaters Waltz - 16 Bar - instrumental
              segue
Chester's Waltz - 1 chorus Vocal male group                               :28
Chester's Waltz - 1 chorus Female and male answers      VOCAL             :30
Meet Me in St. Louis - 1 chorus - instrumental                            :28
Chester's Waltz 1/2 chorus - mixed voices               VOCAL             :21
                                                         Total           2:18
"The Only Girl In The World" - Selection for Charlotte Ballauf (as marked)
     A. "Personality"
     B. "When You're Away"
     C. "March" (as marked)                                              1:45

PRECISION NUMBER:
     A. "College Life" (Intro IX thru - repeat chorus - Dal Segno to verse 2:00
        Play 16 bars of it  cut to chorus and repeat chorus - modulate
        to Wheel.  Built on "College Life" and "Chester's Theme".        1:00
                                                         Total           7:03

TOMMY ALLEN - PATINEUR PRODUCTION - As cut in score                      2:30

HOUND DOG-
     A. Skaters Waltz Galop for entrance as dog is pushed out onto
        ice on sleigh.
     B. "Gleason Theme"
     C. "Java" - Al Hirt
     D. "Gleason Theme" for Exit                                         4:00
                                                    Total Time         13:33

SCENERY:  One roll drop of exterior of Central Park Type of Scene with skating
          pond.  Four carryoffs, including two snow trees.  Carryoffs should be
          two full flats.

PROPS:    Overhead snow machine for opening picture, sixteen pieces or more.
          Sleigh for Hound Dog Number.
          Large Scarf for Hound Dog Number.
          Pipe for Hound Dog Number.
          Ear Muffs for Hound Dog Number.
```

From "the bible" -- the "Production encyclopedia, 1966 Edition of Holiday On Ice", which contained a breakdown of all numbers, call assignments, props, scenery, music, costume inventory, and timing sheet. This is page one: the opening, precision & hound dog numbers.

Sue and Carl Moseley, appearing in a show at Countryside Mall in Clearwater, Florida in the early 1980s. Carl and Sue were married in 1976. They skated, judged, and conducted skating club activities together for two decades.

Chapter Thirty-Five
Memories Are Made of This

We finished a successful engagement of the new *Holiday On Ice* of 1966 (U.S.A.), in Knoxville, TN, and began the short trek to New York, with but two more cities in which to polish and perfect the show, beforehand: Nashville, Tennessee and Johnstown, Pennsylvania.

For extra money and experience, I was beginning to work the move-out and move-in on the baggage car crew, and that first night out of Knoxville, I was driving a jeep, hauling HOI wagons from the Knoxville Civic Center to the rail siding where our HOI "baggage" cars were placed awaiting pick-up, and once fully loaded by an engine, for attachment to the show train.

The heaviest of our 19 wagons were the set, with the beams, etc., that formed the set, and the electric, which held the overhead lighting beams, big strong "follow" spots, and all other lights and sound equipment. The Knoxville building was at the foot of a steep hill that led up to the AJ (Andrew Johnson Hotel) and Main Street. Naturally, one of the first wagons I got to haul was an electric! Two thirds of the way up that hill, my jeep stopped and would go no further, much to my dismay. I was in fear that wagon, jeep and all, would shortly be sliding

"My Story" by Carl Moseley

backwards down that hill, but Butch Collins, who was driving the jeep just behind me, hopped out of his and showed me how, by shifting to a lower gear, to get slowly moving again, up the hill! *"Memories are made of this..."*

The train trip to Nashville was a day trip by coach, with a couple of hours' change over in Chattanooga, before being hooked to another scheduled train on to Nashville. The old station in Chattanooga was large and dusty (before the make-over as "The Chattanooga Choo-Choo"), and the kids congregated to a little bar just across the street from the station for some liquid refreshment. Nancy DeHays Hepburn, reminded me some time back that on this occasion, I bought her first drink at that little bar!

Also, while we were awaiting the train change over, Tommy Collins had me accompany him to where our HOI rail baggage cars were parked, out in the station rail yard to make sure all was secure, and the cars were turned in the right direction for unloading upon arrival!

The building we played in Nashville, the Municipal Auditorium, was still new and a very nice venue for the show. However, on opening night (if I recall correctly), our own sound system failed just as Benny Stabler was conducting the first few notes! I thought, with dismay, that this better not happen in New York! After a short delay, and without our amplified sound and announcements, Benny picked it up and continued to lead the orchestra and guide the show on in that manner. At least that's how I remember it... a painful HOI memory, so maybe I'm painting the brightest side of it! ...

See color photo section: "Picnic in the Kiddy Zoo" photos

Nashville Municipal Auditorium

Chapter Thirty-Six

A Very Unique Mule Act

No discussion of *Holiday On Ice* of 1966 (U.S.A.) would be complete without some remarks about "Kossmayer's Mules"!

Karl Kossmayer joined us with his very unique mule act in Knoxville, and I must tell you that this act evoked a reaction, unequalled by any I have ever seen.

Ronnie Robertson had developed into a master showman and could get maximum audience response, and Tommy Allen Weinreich was certainly a great crowd pleaser, receiving loud "bravos" and whistles on opening night in New York! Similar reactions were common for Tommy with Juanita Percelly, and others, too, but Karl Kossmayer's mules topped them all.

During a Boy/Girl Scout matinee, the scout audience reaction became so overwhelming that it was almost frightening. I kid you not -- the roof of the building in Detroit seemed to be actually shaking! Karl's act was more about him than the mules, in reality. It was a perfect audience spoof, proving that, like in "chasing the wheel", the audience likes to be fooled, and verifying P.T. Barnum's theorem: "There's a sucker born every minute!"

"My Story" by Carl Moseley

Karl and his sister played the part of an ordinary, suited middle-aged audience member and matronly wife, and after three of the "nice little mules" were introduced, and audience folks were invited to ride them, and several fellows had been bucked off (including HOI stooges Jim, "Hoss" Coatney, and Butch Collins, and later, Frank Micale, in a cameo role), Karl would arise from his front row seat, much to the dismay of his "wife," proceed to give it try and attempt to ride the mules.

After a few buckings and kicks, back & forth, between Karl and mule, Karl finally succeeded in riding, prone, backwards, on one of the mules to the glee of the audience! He would then fall on the the ice with his pants coming down, revealing white boxer-shorts, and Karl's "wife" would come after him, also taking a big, skirt-flying spill...Wow!

This was all to the real serious credit of Karl Kossmayer, master animal trainer, who had taught his mules exactly what to do, whatever happened in the act. Not to my knowledge, at the time, Karl was in reality a versatile performer with animals, taking a bow with half a dozen horses! Karl Kossmayer later married Sjoukje Dijkstra Kossmayer, who joined us in New York, and stayed for major cities.

You can see the video of Karl's number on the Ed Sullivan Show, HOI'70: https://www.youtube.com/watch?v=1JsdTkkbC8g :

See color photo section:
Publicity photos in HOI'66 program

KARL KOSSMAYER . . .
One of the oldest and proudest names in the world of entertainment is Kossmayer. The family has been renowned as animal trainers and comedians for several generations. Karl deserted the field of training horses to experiment with mules and has developed one of the funniest and most unusual acts ever seen. These unrideable mules have been the hit of show after show and they're something entirely new for an American skating revue.

Karl Kossmayer's mules on ice & Karl taking a bow with horses in a circus setting

"My Story" by Carl Moseley

Chapter Thirty-Seven

The Show Must Go On

In order to accommodate Karl Kossmayer's Mules, we had to rent, in addition to our three company owned custom "baggage" rail cars, a boxcar that carried Karl's four mules, straw, the young mule groom from Germany, with his bunk and all the cast's trunks, from town to town.

On a trip through Indiana, the boxcar developed a "hotbox" near Terre Haute, and caught fire, including the straw for the mules. A hotbox is a fire caused by friction, etc., in the possibly under-greased wheels and axles. Smoke was pouring out of the boxcar, and in the days before cell phones and walkie-talkies, the mule groom was hanging out the side of the car, trying to get someone else's attention!

Finally, he did. The train was brought to a halt, and a local fire department was called. In the meantime, somehow, wagon master Jim Coatney ("Hoss"), was able to cut a hole in the boxcar wall, with a HOI welding torch, to get at the flames. The local fire-fighters arrived and put a hose through the car hole, finally extinguishing the flames, but the smoke had done its damage, and sadly one of Karl's mules died a few days later from smoke inhalation.

We opened in the next town, nevertheless -- the show must go on.

A little anecdote about HOI General Manager Al Grant... Al could be a man of few words, and on some occasions a bit intimidating. U.S. President Calvin Coolidge was known as "Silent Cal", and for good reason, Al Grant acquired the nickname (but *not* to his face) of "Silent Al."

Lighting director Don Watson, whom I would visit at his post from time to time and chat with during the 10-minute or so mule act (which played with house lights full-up, and no further lighting changes were needed during the number), told me this little story about Al Grant.

Al came in from the Cleveland office, occasionally, to check on things with the show, and on one such occasion, appeared in the lighting booth and seated himself next to Don Watson, just as Karl Kossmayer's 10-minute mule act was about to begin. Don, not to be intimidated by Al Grant and remembering Al's nickname, decided that he, Don Watson, would not be the first to initiate a dialog with Al, and by cranky, the mule act continued in silence (between them), until at the very end, Al Grant got up and walked away, without a word!

In truth, however, Al Grant was a fine fellow, hard-working, and dedicated to the success of *Holiday On Ice*, having paid his dues as a road company manager, etc. before becoming HOI general manager.

The large heavy skirts filled with batteries and lights in the Ted Shuffle "Jubilee" finale are the ones that Jim Coatney, Butch Collins, and I worked as dressers (for $15/show - great money, then). In cities where there were not enough male costume dressers, we got under and held up the skirts for the gals to climb into, and then later retrieved them out on the ice, by pulling in the wet tarps that the gals dropped the skirts onto during the on-ice costume change. We re-hung the big skirts on their racks backstage... showbiz!

You can see the video I filmed of it:
https://www.youtube.com/watch?v=8-_rwAntmyU :

See color photo section:
Jubilee finale

Chapter Thirty-Eight

Best Laid Plans...

The next city (and the last in which to polish the show before New York) was Johnstown, Pennsylvania. In a nutshell, Johnstown was/is a hockey town.

Wikipedia reports: "On May 2, 2015, Johnstown was announced the winner of the 2015 Kraft Hockeyville USA contest and was awarded $150,000 toward improvements of the Cambria County War Memorial Arena. The contest was sponsored through a partnership between Kraft Foods, the National Hockey League (NHL), and National Hockey League Player's Association (NHLPA)."

The show was well received there, and we filled the smallish 4,000 seat Cambria County War Memorial Arena that was built in 1950 -- before the "new" onset of round sports arenas. Johnstown is also remembered for the Johnstown Flood of 1889: The Great Flood of 1889... "occurred on May 31, 1889, after the catastrophic failure of the South Fork Dam on the Little Conemaugh River...With a volumetric flow rate that temporarily equaled that of the Mississippi River, the flood killed 2,209 people and caused US$17 million of damage (about $450 million in 2015 dollars)." We could still see the water marks way up high on downtown brick buildings that survived the flood!

The big attraction otherwise, in Johnstown, was the "Inclined Plane", which took you up a hill (a small mountain, actually), adjoining the city. My wife then, Linda, and I took the ride once, which was enough!

That first time arriving and unloading the show in New York was an experience I will never forget, working the move-in. Let's just say that it proved "Murphy's Law" that "if anything can go wrong, it will."

The plan was to unload the wagons from the baggage rail cars, now parked on a rail siding in Brooklyn, in the pre-dawn hours, so as to beat the morning rush hour traffic coming from the bridge into midtown Manhattan and Madison Square Garden. Joe LeMac's other brother (not Tony or Johnny), whose name escapes me, decided to "help us out" in pulling the wagons from the train. Well meaning, but resulting in a wagon being stuck, wedged against the side of a rail car, stopping all unloading for quite some time, enough to put me and others with jeeps and wagons, inching our way at about 8:00 a.m. across the aforesaid bridge, slowly toward Manhattan and the Garden!

See color photo section:
Johnstown Flood

Johnstown Arena and the Inclined Plane

"My Story" by Carl Moseley

Chapter Thirty-Nine

Last Shows in the Old Garden

I and my other move-in crew members, driving *Holiday On Ice* jeeps and each pulling a HOI wagon, slowly inched our way across the Queensboro Bridge in morning rush-hour traffic toward Manhattan and down to the old Madison Square Garden at 8th Ave. and 49th St.

We were scheduled to open in two days. We opened on a Wednesday, allowing one day to set up the show and one day of special rehearsals.

A new Madison Square Garden was under construction at 33rd St. and 8th Ave. on the site of Pennsylvania Station, whose massive columns and huge, grand waiting room were demolished while the trains kept running below! When we detrained from our passenger cars earlier, huge sheets of visqueen hung, masking off the escalators up from the boarding area from the dust and constant noise of jack hammers, etc.

After negotiating one-way streets and traffic, I finally arrived at the back door of Madison Square Garden and made it out onto the ice with my first wagon -- waiting there were Al Grant, Tommy Collins (sporting an awful head cold with red nose and signature pink shirt), and the crew of local stagehands, under guidance of our department heads, waiting to unload the wagons and set up the show!

The next two years in New York we decided to have our baggage rail cars parked west of the Garden, in town in an area of warehouses and accompanying semi-trailers. This was not without problems, either, at least not for me, as I proceeded to get an axle of one wagon jammed against a curbing (forward, yes; backward, iffy) with a semi- on the opposite side, the driver honking his horn loudly for me to move. Finally, the trucker got out of his cab and jumped in my jeep, and he got it moving!

We set up our office, once the office crates were unloaded, in an office with a private entrance and keyed door, on the 49th Street side of the Garden, with a Ringling Bros. and Barnum & Bailey's plate on the door as it was used by them when they were playing the Garden.

No sooner had we gotten the office set up than an unending parade of HOI veterans, etc. began streaming in, including Everett MacGowan, Arthur Concello (former Ringling General Manager and first triple-ever trapeze artist, now an HOI advisor), both with tons of stories.

The old Madison Square Garden (left) and Pennsylvania Station

*See color photo section:
Advertisement for Holiday On Ice and the new Madison Square Garden*

"My Story" by Carl Moseley

Chapter Forty
The Collins Step

Holiday On Ice of 1966 (U.S.A.) was finally unloaded and set up in the "old" (third, and they were building a forth) Madison Square Garden. Tuesday was set aside for polishing-up rehearsals, with our opening for a three-week stay on Wednesday.

I sat in the stands, with the cast spread about, awaiting call to the ice during the afternoon and evening rehearsals. At some point, when the ice was first open for any and all, I got on to stretch my legs a bit, and I was quite surprised (and honored) when Frankie Sawers, sitting up in the stands next to Chester Hale called me over and asked me to repeat a step for him and Chester! I gladly did, with furbish, this time, a favorite step I had seen Tommy Collins do once, which I like to call "The Collins Step."

Opening day came around, and I will never forget standing in front of Madison Square Garden with my wife, Linda, after an early dinner in a close-by eatery, seeing the name "Holiday On Ice" up in lights on the big marquee and saying to each other, "That's us!" Showtime!

Just before the opening show, Tommy Collins handed me programs and tickets and told me to meet Peggy Fleming and her folks, waiting in the lobby, and escort them to their front row seats. I most certainly did, and Peggy and all were most gracious.

The house lights go down, Benny Stabler picks up his baton, and Chester Hale's Currier & Ives Central Park opening number begins, starring Tommy Allen Weinreich and Charlotte Ballauf.

Here is what I wrote under the video I filmed: "Holiday On Ice of 1966 (U.S.A.) -- Opening production, Currier & Ives Central Park scene staged by Chester Hale, to Les Patineurs; Charlotte Ballauf - solo; Tommy Allen - solo; This was the very first number ever performed by Holiday On Ice in New York City at the old Madison Square Garden. The air was electric on opening night, and the audience responded to Tommy Allen's blur spins with loud 'bravos' and whistles, sending chills up my spine!"

The packed house loved our show, including Ronnie Robertson's spectacular performance, and many of us, as a show business tradition, went to Sardis restaurant next to the New York Times building to await the reviews in the morning edition, which were gratifyingly good! I can taste their canneloni, now!

You can see our opening number online:
https://www.youtube.com/watch?v=LfS3hMxxg4Q

See color photo section:
More program photos

"My Story" by Carl Moseley

Chapter Forty-One

Legends On Ice & On Sawdust

There was an ever-flowing river of former skaters and legendary ice show gypsies coming into our *Holiday On Ice* of 1966 (U.S.A.) office at the old Madison Square Garden, and also backstage, filling the backstage area with skating celebrities at many a performance! ·

Jean Sakovich walked into our office to see Tommy Collins. She had sent Tommy a postcard with a picture of the two of them doing split jumps side-by-side, in years past, under which she had written "Weren't we the greatest!"

Legend Everett McGowan, who with Ruth Mack had been in the very first Ice Capades in New Orleans in 1940, and before that, in Ice Follies of 1939, and who was a good friend of *Holiday On Ice* president Morris Chalfen, came in and visited, fascinating me with his stories! I had seen McGowan & Mack live when my Dad, Carl H. Moseley, promoted Ice Vogues of 1947 ("Little Holiday"), and my dad and Everett became friends, too).

Talk about fascinating stories! Arthur (Art) Concello certainly had them, as he leisured about in our office. Art, wealthy and owner of the Yellow Cab Co. in Sarasota, Florida, was a technical consultant to

Holiday On Ice, having been General Manager of Ringling Bros. and Barnum & Bailey Circus. He designed the portable folding bleachers you see in many gyms and wagons, etc., and was one of the first people to perform a triple somersault under "The Big Top."

According to Wikipedia: "When legendary Alfredo Codona tore a shoulder muscle and retired from the trapeze in 1933, it was the young Arthur Concello who took his place in the centre ring. Concello's act made circus history when his wife Antoinette joined him in performing the triple somersault at Madison Square Garden, New York in 1937, the two performers both attaining the triple to display the highest peak of team flying ever witnessed at that time."

Art told about selling circus tickets -- all cash, and all for each performance, with no advance sales, from the ticket window of the Ringling Bros. office wagon, and filling the floor with same to be later gathered up and stored in a hidden compartment under the wagon. This was all fine until someone got wind of it, and cut a hole in the bottom of the office wagon late one night! Arthur, who wore a pistol belt in those circus days, also told some rather chilling tales about the "roustabouts" who drove the tent stakes, three at a time, in sequence, with sledgehammers!

You can view McGowan & Mack:
http://www.youtube.com/watch?v=2JpFLEn2H84

Arthur Concello in his circus days

"My Story" by Carl Moseley

Jean Sakovich, mid-split!

"My Story" by Carl Moseley

Chapter Forty-Two
Celebrities & Gypsies

As, mentioned earlier, our backstage area at the old Madison Square Garden in New York was a flurry of activity nightly, with celebrities and "gypsies" coming in to visit from all around! The only place on tour where it was busier, and you could hardly move, there, was Pan-Pacific Auditorium in Hollywood!

Famed Howard Nicholson, "Nick", showed up and invited Jimmy Crockett to skate in Nick's upcoming Lake Placid (World) Professional Championships. Jimmy considered, but opted to wait, for several years as it turned out, and entered the Jaca World Pros, which Jimmy Crockett won! Many Ice Capades folks visited us as a stop-over on their way from Atlantic City to New Haven, Connecticut. (They would play New York later in the year.)

Comedian Johnny Labreque, whose partner at that time was George Bussey, hubby to be of Gerty Desjardins Verbiwski, came into the Garden in the afternoon, as I was on the ice getting a little workout, and greeted me for a pleasant, rinkside chat! Phil Romayne was backstage, and we talked for a bit, probably about my past protege, Nancy Isquick (formerly Wallace), who with Ed Mc Cormick had become understudies for Phil Romayne and Cathy Steele Bietak, and then, principals on the just finished Ice Capades Australian tour.

I had called Nancy, home in Florida, from our room at The President Hotel on opening day in New York, enthusiastically suggesting that Nancy and Eddie stop over briefly in New York on their upcoming flight to the Casa Caroica in Garmisch, Germany. Our whole production staff, including HOI Director/Choreographer Chester Hale, were still in New York and could take a peek at Nancy and Eddie for future reference. Airline reservations had already been made, and the Casa and Terry Rudolph awaited, so the rest is history!

After a fruitful, extended time at the Casa Carioca under Terry Rudolph, Nancy Isquick (Wallace) partnered with and later married Alan DiJon of "La Dolce Vita". Anita Ekberg was lifted by Alan in the Trevi Fountain. There were many other films for many successful touring years, worldwide, including an engagement at the Eiffel Tower restaurant in Paris, and Italy's "Circus On Ice."

Ed Mc Cormick met and partnered Christine Jarvis (now Caldwell), Carol Phipson's twin sister, for several very successful years of starring in *Holiday On Ice* Europe! "Fancy" Nancy Isquick found a new partner on Las Vegas ice, with her other skating buds and Kevin Anderson.

You can see a video of Nancy and Eddie:
http://www.youtube.com/watch?v=NGDv499__1A

"Nick" jumping over the ladies

"My Story" by Carl Moseley

*Phil Romayne
&
Cathy Steele
Bietak*

*Nancy Isquick
(Wallace)
&
Eddie McCormick in
the Garden in '64*

Chapter Forty-Three

Great Friendships & Food

Since many of the Ice Capades folks visited us on their way to New Haven, large number of HOI folks rented a bus on our next night off and drove up to see Ice Capades of 1966 at the New Haven Arena!

The Arena was one of the older rectangular buildings, similar to the Philadelphia Arena and the Toledo Arena, and there was very little space backstage, behind the ice. You almost had to walk single file across the back of the backstage ice. I recall Phil Romayne and Cathy Steele Bietak hunched-up against the back wall, making the best of things, while waiting to go on!

We were well-received by the Ice Capades gang, who threw a nice party for us after the show with eats and all. Lots of ice show gypsies visited together that night, and made new, and renewed old, friendships. Mike Burns became quite enamored with one very cute gal, and I wasn't quite sure we were going to get him back on the bus when it was time to leave. Truth be known, had it been me, the bus would have left, and I would have gotten one of the many trains back to New York the next day!

"My Story" by Carl Moseley

Our hotel, in New York, the President, on 49th St. was within short walking distance of the old Madison Square Garden, and close to Broadway theaters, and Radio City Music Hall, in the other direction, which was great, but it was an older hotel, with very narrow corridors, small rooms, and a shaky, iffy, elevator!

Two years later, it was wholly renovated and quite grand on my last stay there for HOI'68. The saving grace of the President Hotel that first year was the chili parlor next door and down under, which served the best chili-con-carne I have ever eaten, and many a night after the show found me, and my wife then, Linda, there, as I lapped it up!

Another plus was the original Mama Leone's restaurant, just across the street, where no one never left hungry (or poor, either). Before you even saw the menu, they put a big block of imported Swiss cheese and some ripe red tomatos, before you on the table. I can rarely get past the spaghetti and meatballs in a good Italian restaurant, and believe me, it was good at Mama Leone's in New York. I had heard rave reviews of it, while working a a waiter in an Italian restaurant in Philadelphia, from a fellow student-waiter! Canelloni at Sardis in New York is my other all-time favorite Italian dish.

Paul and Eva Roman, World Ice Dance Champions, and wonderful folks, joined our show in New York for major cities. You can see their number online:
https://www.youtube.com/watch?v=kDldmomq1mc ,

*See color photo section:
Paul & Eva Roman*

*The President Hotel
in New York*

*Mama Leone's (above)
& "Mama Leone" herself (below)*

Mother was never happier than when she was cooking for friends.

"My Story" by Carl Moseley

Chapter Forty-Four
The Magic Behind the Scenes

During our New York stay with *Holiday On Ice* of 1966 (U.S.A.), Tommy Allen Weinreich married Juanita Percelly at the Actors Chapel at St. Malachy's Church. The ceremony was followed by a fine reception, to which all Holiday On Ice folks were invited, in Tommy and Juanita's Honeymoon Suite, way up in the famous Plaza Hotel, with a grand view of Central Park! A glorious time was had by all!

While walking up toward Broadway for a snack after the show one night, Walter Mathau stepped out of the stage door of the theater where he was playing in "The Odd Couple," and walked on a few steps in front of us, on an otherwise empty street. We did not disturb Walter's reverie!

HOI Stage Manager Joe LeMac's brother, Johnny, after touring with *Holiday On Ice*, became chief electrician (for 30 years) at Radio City Music Hall. Linda and I went to the stage door of Radio City Music Hall one afternoon and asked for Johnny LeMac, who, sure enough, soon appeared and gave us a cook's tour of the Music Hall from top bottom, including a view of the huge three elevators under the stage, used to raise up groups of dancers and whole scenes!

A performance was in progress, and I found myself onstage, just hidden behind a side curtain viewing the Rockettes in their kickline a few feet in front of me. Johnny LeMac certainly extended himself in showing us about that day!

Our chief electrician with *Holiday On Ice*, "IA" (IATSE, International Alliance of Theatrical Stage Employees) union member Merrill Richardson from Miami, whose wife, Kitty Richardson, skated in the show, is a very talented and affable fellow, and his job was arguably one in which the smooth running of each performance depended. Merrill sat at "The Board", the huge control board that Merrill had rebuilt and re-wired by hand in Knoxville once, including hand soldering. In view of the show, he controlled all of the show lights, overhead, surround, and all, except the ten or so "Follow Spots", and changed lighting patterns on cue from Lighting Director Don Watson.

Merrill could pre-set effects on the board and instantly engage the change upon Don Watson's command (after earlier giving Merrill the pattern ID number from Don's lighting manual), over the internal communications system, to "Hit it"! Merrill controlled all the show's sound as well, including the taped vocals inserted at just the right time in Benny Stabler's live orchestra! Wayne Lass followed Merrill Richardson as chief electrician as I remember, and Wayne's wife, Barbara Lass, whom I auditioned, took my wife's place in the show a couple of years later!

The Plaza Hotel

St. Malachy's Church

See color photo section:
Radio City Music Hall

Chapter Forty-Five

Stepping In & Up

Some have asked why Ronnie Robertson "jumped" from Ice Capades to *Holiday On Ice*. There was actually about a two-year gap in-between, so it wasn't really a jump. Every show, sooner or later, needs new stars to keep thing fresh for audiences. Ronnie must have had a seven- or so year contract with Ice Capades -- a long time in this business -- and at the end there must have been reasons, perhaps on both sides, why a renewal wasn't agreed upon.

Holiday On Ice had just been bought by Madison Square Garden Corp. and American Broadcasting Corporation/Paramount Pictures, and HOI was then looking for ways to beef up the show for New York, Hollywood, etc., and a headliner like Ronnie filled the bill. He was available, and HOI signed him for a five-year contract at $50,000.00 per year, the first two years, and $75,000.00 per year each of the last three. That was quite a bit of money in those days!

I was told that Ronnie's contract did not require him to go to Mexico City with us the last 30 days on the tour, which Ronnie opted not to do, for *Holiday On Ice* of 1966. Jimmy Crockett was picked to do Ronnie's numbers for that city. Ronnie personally coached Jimmy Crockett for many nights after the show during the month before Mexico City, on his interpretive "24 Hour" solo, choreographed by Ted Shuffle, and Annie Schmidt worked with Jimmy Crockett afternoons on Ronnie's straight "Gypsy" number.

As Annie and Jimmy were working together, one afternoon, and I was on the ice also, Annie and Jimmy hit a snag on one of Ronnie's steps going back up the ice in the slow, middle section. Remembering it well from watching Ronnie, I did sort of a demonstration for them, which was taken in good faith, and helped to smooth things out.

Jimmy Crockett and I were good friends, and I skated often with Jimmy and Marie Crockett on practice ice, always marveling at Jimmy's blur spins, and Jimmy was always receptive to suggestions for new elements, two steps of which (one "stolen" from Harris Collins) I showed to Jimmy and which he incorporated into his new numbers the next years as the star of *Holiday On Ice* International (U.S.A.).

About that same time, in the Spring of 1966, Wilma Leary came in for a visit to see what she was getting the following year as producer/director, with her hubby, Ed Leary, of *Holiday On Ice* International (U.S.A.). Marie Crockett was interested in securing an understudy, or perhaps principal spot the following year in HOI International. I worked with Marie from films I had made of Charlotte Ballauf (and Tommy Allen Weinreich) in our opening Central Park scene to prepare an audition number to Charlotte's music on tape, which Marie nicely performed for Wilma Leary one afternoon.

I sat next to Wilma as Marie skated. Wilma was most gracious and appreciative, and, as I recall, Marie Crockett did succeed in doing some spots for the Learys in *Holiday On Ice* International (U.S.A.).

Watch Ronnie, in the "Gypsy" number mentioned above:
https://www.youtube.com/watch?v=Cq_zl_J_0EE

See color photo section:
Jimmy Crockett

Holiday On Ice 1965-1968 U.S.A.

Some High Points

Chapter Forty-Six
It Takes Three, Baby

After a very successful New York engagement, we moved on to other large cities. On about the third time around, these cities each became quite familiar, and one almost lost the sense of traveling, but rather like going from home to home, at least for me. Philadelphia, twice, came shortly after New York, and my memory of the "move-in" brings to surface two items. We played the brand new "Spectrum" way down Broad Street, south of the city and near the Philadelphia Airport.

On my first time pulling a *Holiday On Ice* wagon by jeep, down the ramp in back, and into the Spectrum, onto the ice, I noticed sparks falling to the left and right of me. Looking up I saw a couple of fellows with welding torches, working high up near the roof. When I asked Tommy Collins what was going on, he said they were welding another inch or so of steel to the cross beam, that our set would hang from, to be sure that it was strong enough to support the set!

Item two: For the move-in for HOI'67 (luckily the rail siding where our rail baggage cars were parked was less than a mile down the street), for some reason only wagon master Jim Coatney ("Hoss") and I showed up at first, and we set up the ramps to the train and began hauling the wagons, by jeep, to the Spectrum. Well, in taking down

"My Story" by Carl Moseley

the 20' or so rolled up "picture sheet" (which was used in a rear screen projection of Petra Burka at Worlds), the thing bent in half, to our surprise and dismay, as it needed a third person to support it at its mid-point! No picture-sheet for Philadelphia! But Petra skated just fine, anyway!

Jimmy Grogan, who then was teaching at The Philadelphia Skating Club & Humane Society (PSC&HS), brought a group of his pupils and visited backstage, and some of my old skating buddies from the PSC&HS, the Philadelphia Arena, and the International Skating Club of Philadelphia showed up, including Jo Ann Ferguson and Joel Leeds ("Gus").

Ronnie Robertson had performed pristinely in New York, pleasing everyone, but it was my luck that on the matinee day that Jo Ann and Gus were in the audience, Ronnie was quite unhappy, as someone had gotten into his dressing room the night before and stolen his TV! Of course, Tommy Collins was away that day on other HOI business, and as assistant company manager, the buck stopped with me!

Performance director Annie Schmidt came up to me and said: "Carl, you've got to go talk to Ronnie -- He says he's not going to skate this show. *Gulp!* Well, I still don't know what I said, but I got up my courage and went into Ronnie's dressing room, and must have said the right thing, in empathizing and appealing, as in the end Ronnie agreed to go on, after all!

However, I suppose he was still rather upset, since his performance was, as they say, after a fashion. As I was sitting in the stands with my friends, Jo Ann and Gus, watching the matinee, Ronnie Robertson came on for his first number, and proceeded to do single waltz jumps, throughout! Ronnie did do his famous spins, however. At least, I hope so. I was too stunned to remember! I could only look at Jo Ann and Gus in wonder, but they just laughed it off!

Ronnie was not unreliable in the least... he just had an artistic temperament, as is often the case with creative and talented stars.

The Spectrum (above)
The Famous Rocky Statue (right)
&
the Ben Franklin Hotel (below)

"My Story" by Carl Moseley

Chapter Forty-Seven
Skivvies & The Ghost

Henceforth, in my little story of touring with *Holiday On Ice* 1965-1968, as assistant company manager (and chief cook and bottle washer), I will hit on high points of the 30 cities we visited on each tour, so as not be repetitive and perhaps, mundane.

No one could have skated in a more exemplary manner than Ronnie Robertson. In spite of the rather choppy and brittle ice that other principals were negotiating as best they could, on the day that Ice Follies came to visit in Toledo, Ohio, and Donald Jackson was sitting in the front row, Ronnie pulled out all the stops, including an extra Arabian or two!

Not known by many, maybe, Ronnie Robertson's more guiding attribute was as an absolute cut-up! When Tommy Collins and Janie threw a "come as you are" party in Tommy's hotel suite in Indianapolis, Ronnie did just that, arriving in his white skivvies, while many of us were in our more conservative pajamas.

Guy Longpre and Ivor Robson used a "flat" (piece of background scenery), in their comedy number resembling a jail, with a little barred window up high above the trap doors, below through which they made their exit, and often Ronnie's head would appear in that window making all sorts of faces and grimaces at Guy and Ivor as they approached their exit, and Ronnie was waiting to go on.

Someone, rumored to be Ronnie Robertson, was leaving little notes attached to one of the set supports that said "I love you, The Ghost", purportedly for the benefit of an unknown performer on the ice or about to go on.

We, *Holiday On Ice*, played the vaulted "Winterland", the home of Ice Follies in San Francisco, a building in which the show played well and looked good, but which had no Zamboni. Our Zam wouldn't fit through the back door of Winterland, so the ice had to be resurfaced by hand, with scrapers and squeegee, which left only a passable new sheet of ice.

One afternoon, during Ronnie Robertson's practice time, the ice was rather rough, and worse, quite hard and brittle. Ronnie saw me, and calling me over, asked me if I could do anything about the ice condition, so I sought out the Winterland building engineer, who came out and stood by the ice, and to whom I voiced our concerns about the ice. The building engineer said, bluntly: "This ice is good enough for Ice Follies," to which Ronnie rejoined, "Well, it may be good enough for Ice Follies, but I'm the best skater in the world, and it's not good enough for me!"

You can view a brief video of Ronnie and Alfredo Mendoza in the "24 Hour" fight scene:
https://www.youtube.com/watch?v=Ga8-wgTvbjk

See color photo section: More photos of Ronnie Robertson

Tommy Allen Weinreich & Ronnie Robertson

"My Story" by Carl Moseley

Chapter Forty-Eight
Comedy & Tragedy

There's a little more about Ronnie Robertson's humor... and me. In San Francisco, at "Winterland", on New Year's Eve 1965, Edy DeVos, a former *Holiday On Ice* skater who ran a catering service catered for us between shows. He invited the cast to his condo apartment with an outside deck and fountain for a New Year's Eve party after the show. I came to the show dressed in a suit for the party, but was soon asked to portray "Father Time" with Ronny LeMac as "Baby New Year" in the Finale, that night.

Wardrobe Mistress Connie Gardner fixed me up with a sheet, a fake cotton beard, and a white wig, and down the ice Ronny LeMac and and came at the end of the Finale, to stand and pose in the center of the principals' line-up. While the lights were still up, Ronnie Robertson, who was standing next to me, turned and laughingly tried to pull my sheet off me! He probably assumed I had a dance belt or less underneath, but the move kinda' fizzled as was all that was revealed was my nice suit. That was Ronnie!

In the early Fall, we played Indianapolis at the Fairgrounds Coliseum. On Halloween night 1963, during the finale of *Holiday On Ice* of 1964 (U.S.A.), there was an explosion caused by propane leaking from a concession popcorn popper under the stands. The explosion lifted a whole section of stands into the air and onto the ice, killing 60-plus people, and injuring 200! As tragic as it was, it was also miraculous, as no skater nor anyone with *Holiday On Ice* was killed, largely due to the position of the "wheel" in the finale. It was a night no one there will ever forget. Two years later, playing the Indianapolis Coliseum, folks who had been there felt creepy in the building!

Lucy Carpenter, told me that, as assistant performance director, she had been standing in the aisle next to where the explosion occurred, watching and making correction notes, when stage manager Joe LeMac called out to her, "Lucille, come backstage - we need you back here" just before the explosion!

Enough has been posted elsewhere about the gory details, so I'll forego any more remarks about that here and go on with a least one pleasant remembrance of Indianapolis (besides Tommy and Janie's come-as-you-are party, mentioned earlier), and that was seeing and chatting with a friend of old, Ronny Ludington, who I first met at the U.S. National Roller Skating Championships in 1951.

Ronny was teaching in Indianapolis, and we allowed him some ice time with a group of his pupils. Some of us came on the ice to skate, and Ron came on out, too, showing that he could still do a jump or two. A group also liked to skate some nights after the show, wherever we were. The downside of the Indianapolis building, however, was the building engineer, who (with blinders on) came out and turned off the building lights saying to us: "There never has been any skating after the show, and there never will be!" I forget how we resolved that.

See color photo section:
The Ice Follies at the Winterland Program, 1941 and the one and only Ronnie Robertson

"My Story" by Carl Moseley

Winterland, just before demolition (above) & the Indianapolis Fairgrounds Coliseum (right)

Chapter Forty-Nine

A Really Big Shew

When *Holiday On Ice* of 1966 played "Maple Leaf Gardens" in Toronto, Sheldon Galbraith, who had taught Harris Collins, came in to our show office for a visit with Tommy Collins, and I met Sheldon.

Sheldon and his brother, Murray Galbraith, whom I had seen many times (and idealized) as the star of *Holiday On Ice*, had previously starred as a shadow pair in Ice Follies. As the Toronto folks were huge fans of their "Maple Leafs" hockey team, and there was a game on Saturday night, we had to move most of the HOI show stuff out in back of the building, and then back in again, for our closing performances on Sunday.

Before each show at Maple Leaf Gardens, "God Save The Queen" was played, and there was a huge portrait of Queen Elizabeth II.

Our second year in New York, *Holiday On Ice* of 1967 (U.S.A.), was highlighted by a taping for *The Ed Sullivan Show* -- as Ed would say, "A Really Big Shew." A pre-taping technical meeting was scheduled in a small room in the old Madison Square Garden, into which crammed anybody who could possibly be connected with the taping. I was there to see what was going on.

"My Story" by Carl Moseley

There was an endless discussion of light levels, "Kelvins", etc., with this early taping in color. In the end, it looked to me as if they just used our normal show lighting, but big floods were strewn about the balcony railings, needed or not.

We had an all-day taping session for groups, etc., and then in the evening Ronnie Robertson's and Tommy Allen Weinreich & Juanita Percelly's performances were taped live, straight through! A good bit of time was spent in the afternoon taping some of Eric Waite's moves, but none was used in the final broadcast, as was none of the Marine precision number, or the chorus gal's "pussy cat" group number.

I captured these in my candid filming of the day. Watch the video closely, and you will see "Clown Prince of the Ice" Eric Waite approach Ed Sullivan expecting a handshake, but Ed was absorbed in other technical matters:

Notice Holiday On Ice president Morris Chalfen shaking hands with Ed Sullivan (below), and Holiday On Ice Vice-President Eugene Pleshette, and Mr.C with Ed (left)

See color photo section:
The Maple Leaf Garden
&
Screen shot of Ronnie Robertson with Ed Sullivan

Chapter Fifty

Reno Gals, Oakland Woods

Holiday On Ice of 1966 (U.S.A.), as in many years, celebrated Thanksgiving in Des Moines, Iowa. This year, we celebrated in the midst of a white-out snow storm, but with an elegant Thanksgiving dinner with all the trimmings served between shows, in a room at the building.

In the lobby of our hotel, I ran into comedian Hennie Youngman, who was also performing in Des Moines, and invited him to the show. He thanked me, but I'm not sure if he showed up.

We closed the first half of the tour in Reno, Nevada, staying at the historic Riverside Hotel & Casino. The hotel was next to the river into which divorcees conventionally dumped their wedding rings, and sported a revue with some dazzling gals, one of whom, our drummer, Skip Pittman, became enamored with, rumor has it!

Skip and HOI percussionist Dave Wilson would, on occasion, get back up on the bandstand and jam after the show, as some of us were getting in some skating on the ice -- it kept us moving!

We played the new, Centennial Coliseum in Reno, and on closing night, Tommy Collins and I had a drink at the bar in the building, and

"My Story" by Carl Moseley

chatted with Murray Galbraith, former *Holiday On Ice* star, who was currently working as a dealer in Reno! There I sat, happily, with two of my skating idols.

We closed the first half of the tour the next year, with *Holiday On Ice* of 1967 (U.S.A.), at the new Oakland-Alameda County Coliseum, in Oakland, California, and my mom and dad flew in to San Francisco to join me and my wife, Linda, for the last shows in Oakland, and then, with a rental car, a vacation week tour of Northern California.

Our tour included the Muir Woods in Sausalito and a northern Italian restaurant in San Francisco (seeking canelloni to match Sardis's -- not quite). With my folks, we skipped the hot spots we had visited the year earlier featuring the "pole dance" and other such like attractions, but we did pop up to Reno for fantastic steaks before driving on down to San Diego for a Christmas Day opening at another new building.

My folks flew back to Florida from San Diego, but not before we enjoyed some great seafood and a nice New Year's dinner party for all arranged by the show and Tommy Collins. It was on a paddle wheeler on the bay by the Bahia Hotel where we were staying. Skee Goedhart's parents were there, and Tommy Collins seated my folks with them on the boat for dinner. Later that night, a riotous and memorable party took place in a room at our hotel; my folks opted to skip, thankfully.

Learn all about the Riverside Hotel:
http://renohistorical.org/items/show/3?tour=5&index=3

*See color photo section:
Reno, Nevada*

Murray Galbraith, one of the author's idols

The Riverside Hotel in Reno, Nevada

"My Story" by Carl Moseley

Chapter Fifty-One
Sonja and Other Stars

There is so much to say about playing Pan-Pacific Auditorium in Hollywood, *Holiday On Ice* of 1967 (U.S.A.)! Visitors to the show, gypsies and legends alike, exceeded our New York engagement, and it was almost difficult to move about backstage, night after night!

Don Watson introduced me to Larry Jackson of Jackson & Lynam, long-time Ice Capades comedians. (Larry was also "Papa Bird" in the 1939 movie with Irene Dare). Larry was working our show as a local IATSE stagehand and was vey cordial. 1940's comedian Kenny Lamb showed up, announcing he was ready for a come-back, as was legend Red McCarthy, who came to Pan-Pacific one afternoon in hopes of skating for Morris Chalfen.

Neither Mr. C nor Tommy Collins were in the office (conveniently, perhaps), so I told Red go on down to the ice, and I would watch him. I was amazed that Red in his 50's could still fly around that huge ice (300 ft. in front of the set -- longest on tour, or anywhere), still doing his jumps from and into spread eagles, etc.! Mr. C greeted Red McCarthy that evening at the show, and bought some exercise equipment from Red that he was selling at his work-out studio, thus smoothing things over.

Bob Gaylor and Rosita Percelly were backstage (married at that time). Tony Curtis and Janet Leigh watched the show from front row seats, on opposite sides of the ice, one with daughter Jamie Lee Curtis, and the other with daughter Kelly.

Into our show office, for visits, came Suzanne Pleshette, daughter of *Holiday On Ice* vice-president Eugene Pleshette, as did one-time HOI show pianist and now Hollywood composer/conductor, Artie Kane, looking spiffy in his black patent leather shoes. Tommy Collins introduced me to legend Mabel Fairbanks in our show office, who had brought a group of her students to see the show. Tommy also introduced me to Ice Capades president Dick Palmer, as he and Dick chatted, watching the show, from an aisle.

For our opening night gala, with red carpet, canopy, and searchlights -- the works --attended by ABC/Paramount movie stars, we presented a life-time achievement trophy to Sonja Henie at intermission. A gala reception and party was held after the opening show and attended by the movie personalities, including Buddy Ebsen with his daughter, HOI skater Alix Ebsen, and Eric Waite talking to the "Skipper" of the Minnow, Alan Hale, Jr.!

Don Watson introduced me to Sonja Henie a few days later during exclusive morning ice time we had set aside for her to work on a planned TV comeback. Sonja, who had been waltzing with partner of old, Eugene Mickler, to music from "Dr, Zhivago" on Don's record player, gave us a private exhibition of her new bent-knee spinning ability.

See video links:
https://martinostimemachine.blogspot.com/…/pan-pacific-audit…
https://www.youtube.com/watch?v=e1Xl1QQimXo&feature=related :

"My Story" by Carl Moseley

Line captain Roger Bathurst, holding the trophy, with Sonja Henie and Tommy Collins

Two legends together, Sonja Henie with Ronnie Robertson

Buddy Ebsen with his daughter, HOI skater Alix Ebsen

Alan Hale, Jr. (the famous skipper of the Minnow on the "Gilligan's Island" TV show, mingling with Eric Waite (right) and cast members (below)

Chapter Fifty-Two

Hooray for Hollywood

While in Hollywood, with *Holiday On Ice* of 1967 (U.S.A.), at Pan-Pacific Auditorium, Tommy Collins and I had sandwich lunches with Ice Capades publicity head and Joe LeMac look-alike, Jack Sydney, at the famous Hollywood Farmer's Market, within close walking distance of Pan-Pacific Auditorium. Jack had been an "advance man" (as was Jim Oshust, once way back) for *Holiday On Ice*, and was a very interesting fellow to talk with, having many showbiz tales!

HOI stage manager Joe LeMac and wife, Alice Quessy, must have had connections with the Disney organization, as Alice and Ronny LeMac were invited for a free, escorted tour of Disneyland, and Alice extended the invitation to my wife, Linda, and me, to join them. Join them we did, for an all-day outing at Disneyland, personally escorted to all the best attractions by a representative of "Walt." Quite an eye-opener, with the new "audio-animation" of the Tiki (bird) House, and the Hall of the Presidents!

Also, while in Hollywood, ABC affiliate Channel 7 videotaped our entire show for local broadcast later, and spent nearly a week around the show, familiarizing themselves with the numbers and directing the kids in some cases regarding their presentation for television. The TV director even coached me, as the "popcorn gag" stooge, in Guy Longpre and Ivor Robson's comedy number, as to how he wanted me to react and present. Our show, I understand, was aired more than once in the LA area, and I surely wish I could get access to those tapes if they still exist. I have inquired, but no luck so far.

We were pretty much sold out the last week at Pan-Pacific Auditorium in Hollywood (the last ice show to play there, I believe), and as the last Sunday matinee began, Tommy Collins told me to go out in front of the building and tell the long lines of people waiting in front of the ticket windows that there were no more seats (and no further chance to see our show, either, in effect).

I had another rehearsal period in Knoxville, another stay in New York, and two more visits to Mexico City ahead of me (three in each case, total) before the end of my days on four *Holiday On Ice* tours.

Videos of Tommy Allen Weinreich & Ronnie Robertson in *Holiday On Ice* of 1967 (U.S.A.):
https://www.youtube.com/watch?v=ZBHCwx-fLt0
https://www.youtube.com/watch?v=-999KiH7dkQ

See color photo section:
The Pan-Pacific Auditorium,
Disneyland Castle, and
Hollywood Farmer's Market

Chapter Fifty-Three

From the Ice to the Prairie

We are coming to a close of my stories of happenings during my tours with *Holiday On Ice* of 1965-68 (U.S.A.), but there are a few more topics of possible interest.

When I was running all the Jr. Club sessions (a thousand kids of all ages) at the Philadelphia Skating Club & Humane Society, a few years before joining *Holiday On Ice*, there was this gal in the high school group who was quite animated and loved to give me a bit of trouble, in a friendly manner, from time to time. Her name was Lucy Flippin, and you can imagine how surprised I was when Lucy Lee Flippin showed up for rehearsals in Knoxville for *Holiday On Ice* of 1966 (U.S.A.)!

Lucy Flippin and I renewed our "friendship" of old and actually worked on a few pair moves on practice ice together that year, with perhaps developing a novelty pair number on the order of "The Beattys," but Lucy's future lay in Hollywood, and after that one HOI tour, Lucy Lee Flippin was on her way westward to appear in many episodes of "Little House On The Prairie" and as a dance judge in the movie *Flashdance*. Good for Lucy!

When we played rainy Portland, Oregon before leaving the West Coast, I met, with pleasure, the box office manager of the Portland Coliseum, former *Holiday On Ice* star, Jimmy Lawrence! I had seen Jimmy skate with his partner/wife Margaret Field in *Holiday On Ice* of 1959 (U.S.A.). I had idolized his beautiful, smooth, imaginative footwork!

Jimmy and Margaret also starred in Ice Capades for many years. While in Portland, a small group, including Ron Basten and me, checked out the famous raucous "Barbary Coast" night spot, where there was a "Chastity Belt" on display -- lots of fun, there, that night!

In leaving Portland to go back East, we took "The Empire Builder" cross-country train for a two-day, sight-filled trip to icy Chicago, with ice hanging off the sides of the rail cars as we pulled into the station to be met personally by HOI travel agent Marshall Alderson, who helped us gather our luggage for the bus trip on to Milwaukee.... brrr!

The move-ins and -outs there and in Minneapolis were brutal, in windy dark train sheds, but there were great steaks in Milwaukee. In order to get some ice time in Milwaukee, I emulated, to an extent "ghosts of the arena" idols Alan Konrad and Don Watson, by going to the empty building early Sunday morning (in spite of the long two-show day and "move-out" following).

The cleaning ladies were sweeping the aisles in the semi-dark building, lighted only by work lights, but the rough ice was free! You've got to really want to skate to brave it for a couple of blocks past frozen storefronts early on a freezing windy morning in Milwaukee. We would shortly be on our way back south to Atlanta, the South, and Florida, before we were off to Mexico City, again.

See videos of Jimmy Lawrence & Margaret Field, and not meaning to be hubris, of me (for the record, here, in practice) and in a couple of performance shots:
https://www.youtube.com/watch?v=g-XoMC04WTs
https://www.youtube.com/watch?v=B8_8K71dsXA
https://www.youtube.com/watch?v=v7YlgFcrkNw

See color photo section:
Barbary Coast & The Empire Builder

"My Story" by Carl Moseley

Lucy Lee Flippin,
Holiday On Ice skater and
Hollywood star

The author,
Carl Moseley

Jimmy Lawrence &
Margaret Field

Chapter Fifty-Four

Landing Your Axel in the Front Row...

Having finally left the frozen mid-West in the dead of winter, we moved once more into the warm South and Florida, to soon play the old Municipal Auditorium in Atlanta (the only playable building, there, before the Omni, and later the Phillips Arena).

The Municipal Auditorium was an intimate venue, close-up audience-wise, but our portable ice surface there was the shortest on tour, only about 100 ft. to the front row, into which Ray Balmer tumbled opening night in the process of landing his huge "floater" axel!

The ice length came as quite a shock to most after so recently playing the longest ice on tour, Pan-Pacific Auditorium in Hollywood, with 300 ft. in front of the set. We packed them in that Atlanta Auditorium, and when my aunt, Edith Brown, and cousin Mary Gilbert from Rome, Georgia, came to visit on Saturday, I had to set up folding chairs in an aisle (a no-no, but overlooked) up in the balcony, in order for them to see the show!

Line captain Lucy Carpenter had left the show a month or so earlier to marry Earl Smith in Salt Lake City, and I was more than surprised

"My Story" by Carl Moseley

when, in our huge upstairs office in the Atlanta building, across the large expanse, on opening day, came walking in none other than Lucy!

Tommy Collins knew in advance that Lucy was coming back and had made a veiled, teasing reference in the office about same just a bit earlier. After Lucy showed up, and we all shared mutual surprise greetings, Tommy told Butch Collins and me not to say anything to anybody about Lucy's return, as she planned to just walk into the dressing room, un-announced, for the show that night and start lacing up her skates. Lucy did just that-- to the puzzlement of our amazed cast!

Henceforth, Lucy Carpenter kept a picture of her dad by her bed, under which she had written the caption, as if from her dad, "Don't get married!" as rumor has it.

Video of Ray Balmer, in HOI'67:
https://www.youtube.com/watch?v=e-6sF0CHD_o

The Atlanta Municipal Auditorium

Lucy Carpenter & friends at our Hollywood Opening

*See color photo section:
Yvonne Conley & Sandy Wirwill at the Hollywood Opening Gala and Ray Balmer; Also, an open letter from a fan that all show skaters might want to read!*

My dad, Carl H. Moseley, was the local promoter in Tampa for the first three *Holiday On Ice* productions in Florida: Ice Vogues of 1947 & 1948, and *Holiday On Ice* of 1948. Co-producer of Ice Vogues of 1947, Everett McGowan of "McGowan & Mack", after splitting with Holiday On Ice, Inc., called my father, and offered him a piece of his own show if my dad's building, shown below, could be used for rehearsals of McGowan's new show. My father's 50/50 partner in the Coliseum was more concerned about water from the ice leaking onto the Coliseum's hard rock maple floor, however, so that was the end of that!

The Davis Islands Coliseum in Tampa, Florida, which housed the largest roller skating rink in the South, and where Ice Vogues of 1947 played.

McGowan & Mack
Video of their "Cafe de Apache" number re-enacted in Ice Vogues of 1947:
https://www.youtube.com/watch?v=CVNxfzszRis

Chapter Fifty-Five

Elegant Costumes & Fond Memories

Rita Lowery, a friend to many, many skaters, was a wonderful *Holiday On Ice* skater and coach. She dropped into our show office during *Holiday On Ice* of 1967 (U.S.A.) when we visited to the Hara Arena near Dayton, Ohio. The Hara Arena was/is located in an apple orchard, and according to Wikipedia, "(t)he site was originally the family-owned fruit orchard of Harold and Ralph Wampler. The name stems from HA from Harold and RA from Ralph."
It was a neat and clean, if somewhat remote, building.

Rita greeted Tommy Collins with enthusiasm, and proceeded to show us many pictures from a recent show she and Dave Lowery had recently produced there, featuring elegant costumes loaned to them, I believe, from Ice Follies' wardrobe storage. Rita was very proud of this, and rightly so -- indeed, some of the costumes rivaled ours of the day. Rita also talked enthusiastically about the success of her many skating students, and how much she enjoyed teaching them!

A few years later, I had occasion to send to Dave and Rita a box of extra programs I had. They had a skating memorabilia site on the net, featuring programs, etc. Dave had asked me if I had any from England, Rita's home, as she had none from the special shows produced there, so I included several, such as "Jack & The Beanstock On Ice", etc. Dave told me Rita was thrilled to have them, at last! I told Dave that the programs were gratis, and for them to sell at no charge from me, but Dave sent me a nice gift card that Sue and I used for an equally nice dinner out. Rita passed away while I was working on these stories.

View a great video of Rita and Dave's wonderfully talented daughter Kristan Lowery (Waggoner, now) and great partner, Chip Rossbach. and also a link about the Lowerys and the Hobart Arena in Troy, Ohio:
https://www.youtube.com/watch?v=5kE-AMsU7jY
http://troyhistorymatters.blogspot.com/.../world-of-skating-a...

Dave & Rita Lowery

Program page from Holiday On Ice of 1959 (U.S.A.) with David Lowery as the "Tin Man"

"My Story" by Carl Moseley

Chapter Fifty-Six
Student Successes

Before I wrap up my ramblings about being on tour with Holiday On Ice (U.S.A.) 1965-1968, I want to be sure to mention the great gals whom I coached, and who also were on tour with me in those days!

Susan Comrie (Mrs. Jody Fain) & Eilene Meredith Leibensperger (whom Linda Moseley coached before HOI)

Cheri Check Hollingworth, who understudied Alice Quessy and others

Second from left in the dark suit in the marching picture, Dottie McKenna, also an understudy

I also coached each of these fine skaters who performed with Ice Capades:

Julie Fehr Heinicka

Nancy Isquick (Wallace), who understudied Cathy Steele Bietak

Promo video for HOI'67, showing the Marine drill practice in Tampa:
https://www.youtube.com/watch?v=NDNCXanBtJI

Video of Frank Whidden and Carl Moseley:
https://www.youtube.com/watch?v=MF2-eZtA-V0

Frank Whidden

"My Story" by Carl Moseley

Before Holiday On Ice 1965-1968

Falling In Love with the Ice

"My Story" by Carl Moseley

Chapter Fifty-Seven

Barefoot Boy from the South

I grew up for a few years in a magical place called Indian Rocks Beach. Although I went to grammar school through the third grade at a city school named, ironically, after the fellow who invented the first ice making machine, Gorrie School, in Tampa, my fourth and fifth grades were at a very "country" Anona School, just across the inland waterway from Indian Rocks Beach, where I went to school barefoot, summer and winter!

My dad, Carl H. Moseley, practiced law in Tampa, but when World War II began, he and my mom decided to rent rooms in our big Tampa house to G.I.'s stationed at MacDill AFB, and my Mother, sister, Martha, and I moved over to one of our cottages at Indian Rocks for the duration of the war. Dad would come over on the bus from Tampa for week-ends.

Indian Rocks Beach was, in those days, and even somewhat now, a nature's untouched realm that's hard to imagine -- just a natural adventureland ripe for exploration by kids like myself and my buddies. Mangroves, huge vine-like plants with root structures that weaved in and out through the back-wash mud on the bay side of the island abounded and were a challenge to navigate through, barefoot, with the sandy mud oozing between one's toes while on the lookout for moccasins or other snakes!

On the Gulf side of the island, the beach was endless, natural, and ever inviting, rain or shine, in all of its moods. Sea oats were abundant, with a few Australian pines for shade. I found an abandoned rowboat on the shore and hauled it up from the surf to the drier beach area, and in the days following, caulked the huge gaps in its structure, and painted the bottom with copper-red barnacle-resisting paint. We had a boat to paddle out a few yards, anchor, and fish in!

That old boat, the author's sister Martha, the author, and cousin "Skipper"?

The author and that abandoned rowboat that he found and restored

We had this huge natural beach on the Gulf side of the island, and the backwater mangrove jungle on the intercoastal/bay side. The North mile or so of "Sand Key", across a channel from Clearwater Beach, was completely undeveloped, with no road at all, just waiting to be explored!

Our little cottage was one of the first built on Indian Rocks, and there were several vacant lots adjacent, which proved a playground, too, for us kids. We dug a hideout in the high ground, which we covered with boards, some sand, grass, and a trap door. We camped out there at night with a tent made from blankets, and we made a little fire outside to roast some "weenies," heat canned food, and toast marshmallows.

Unfortunately, on a planned overnight stay our "tent" caught fire from a candle, and I had to run down to the water's edge with the blanket to put it out! In doing so, one of my thumbs was thoroughly blackened by the flames. My tent buddy picked his stuff, and went home, close by, for the night, but I was determined to stick it out under the stars, and lay there with my paining thumb, until finally the sky to the East became gray, signaling dawn and my permission to go home!

Another time, we decided to explore the North end of the island by night, and after walking as far as we could on the beach, we worked our way, barefoot, through the tangled mangroves and mud (and maybe snakes) at the end, until we could finally see the lights of Clearwater Beach on the other side of the channel. There's a big bridge there, now, of course, and a public beach, but we saw it as it really was, once... "Paradise Lost," indeed!

Our first cottage at Indian Rocks Beach

Chapter Fifty-Eight
A Trip Up McKay Creek

The intercoastal waterway separating Indian Rocks Beach from the "mainland" Pinellas County, Florida widened out, forming a bay maybe 3/4 mile wide, not too far from our beach cottages. There were several small islands in that bay, with mangroves and even a few Australian pines. Using a flat-bottom boat from an Army/Navy Surplus store, we visited them, camping out overnight on one. We heated up our canned beans and even scrambled some eggs for breakfast over our little campfire. I sported a small single-shot .22 rifle, and one of my friends, Billy, had a "4/10" shot pistol, and I remember taking a shot at a rabbit in the Palmettos.

Well, one day the three of us got brave and decided to cross the bay to explore McKay Creek, on the mainland side. We shoved off from the island of Indian Rocks Beach in the a.m., crossed the bay, and headed up the mouth of undeveloped "McKay Creek." The water was clear, and we got up perhaps 1/4 of a mile, easily, spotting birds and other wildlife along the way. So far so good, until we realized the creek was getting shallower for some reason.

The tide was going out, and before we knew it our flat-bottomed boat was sitting high and dry on the creek bed... stranded! We realized that we were just stuck until the tide came back in again, so we made the most of it, sunbathing on the sandy creek bottom. This was fine, until a little snake (Billy said it was a rattler) showed up, which Billy destroyed with his shot pistol.

By late afternoon, we finally noticed that there was some water in the creek, once more, so as soon as we could dislodge our boat from the bottom and were afloat, we began to make our way back down to the creek mouth and then into the bay. Soon it was dark, however, and with only flashlights, we began to worry if we could find our way back to the island of Indian Rocks Beach, and our mooring place.

I doubt if we had told our parents much about what we were up to that day, but when it became dark, without our showing up, they, in turn, became concerned (to say the least), and had the temerity to have neighbors turn on dockside floodlights. As soon as we spotted these lights, we headed right toward them, and home... and lived to tell about it, another day!

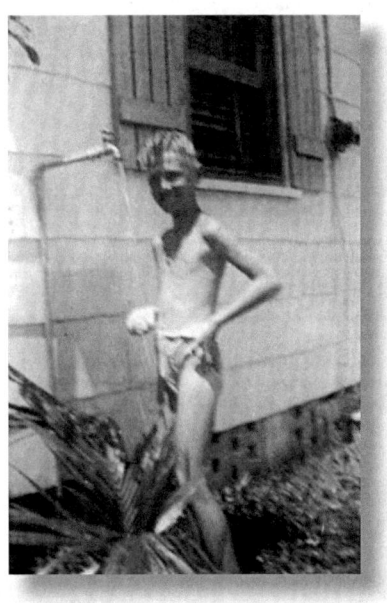

The author cooling off at a spigot outside the family cottage

Chapter Fifty-Nine

Preserving History

The Indian Rocks Beach Historical Museum was once our second beach cottage, in which my sister Martha and I spent the World War II years of 1944 and 1945. I painted those shutters more than once, mowed the big two-lot sandy site with first a heavy rotary push mower (whew!) and later rotary power mower.

Years later, in remodeling it for rental, I sanded the wooden floors and re-finished them with clear plastic coating. Sue, Eric Moseley, and I painted the whole interior then, too. The house was the second at the beach built by my dad, Carl H. Moseley, and it was built largely from lumber purchased in Tampa from a house being torn down there. I remember visiting the demolition site, with my dad, on rainy day, and my father enquiring if the rain was helping with the dismantling, to which he was emphatically answered, "No"!

We took the school bus to the mainland two-room Anona School, where at recess we played barefoot soccer on a dirt field or built hide-out "huts" in the palmetto and scrub oak woods behind the school-house. Another boy and I volunteered to walk a half mile down to the store at the nearest intersection to pick up the bread for the kitchen and treat ourselves to some penny candy! We also tended a "victory garden" at Anona School, with cabbages to sugar cane, which was sweet to chew, upon harvesting.

During those war years, a "blackout" was enforced at the beach, and our cottage, had blackout curtains on all the windows on the beach side. If any light was allowed to escape, there would soon be a knock on the door from a Coast Guard beach patrol member, patrolling the beach, to enforce the after dark curfew. This was for protection, so that any possible German subs in the Gulf would see no shore lights, providing them with an easy target to shell or attack! There were no night bonfires on the beach for parties and weenie roasts in those days... but there were plenty later on.

Indian Rocks Beach is well protected these days, under the guidance of my nephew, Mayor R.B. Johnson, who commanded a major beach replenishment program through the years, restoring sea oats, grasses, and sand dunes... and some crabs and turtles, too!

The family's second Indian Rocks Beach cottage in the 1940s (above)

See color photo section:
Cottage converted to Indian Rocks Beach Historical Museum

Chapter Sixty
First Pair of Ice Skates

Taking the ice, before Holiday On Ice... In 1951, I qualified for the U.S. Nationals on rollers, in Cleveland, Ohio, with Gold in Novice Pairs and Senior Fours at the Southern U.S. Championships, but my Pairs and Fours partners' parents could not afford to send my partner, Carlene Beatty (and they needed her to work in the small motel they owned in Tampa). I hitched a ride, anyway, to go and see the sights and try to feel a part of things.

There, I met Ronny Ludington, friend of my boy Fours partner, Henry Haffke, and I remember Ron and Henry taking turns in the center, trying to out do each other in a public session, Ronny doing Double Axel-Double Mapes (toe loop) combinations! I could do a decent Axel on rollers, and pull out a Double Toe Loop, if I had to, but I was mightily impressed with Ron and all I saw there!

I then drove the car for the lady who had brought us to Cleveland on to New York City, where I was to take a bus to visit Henry in Chicopee Falls, Massachusetts, but I had an hour or two before the bus. I used that time to go down the street to the Roxy Theater to see Arnold Shoda for the first time! All I can say is "Wow!" I had never seen such long spins!

After a week at Henry Haffke's house in Massachusetts with skating every night, I went back to New York, where my dad met me at the New Yorker Hotel for a week in New York, Atlantic City, and Washington, D.C.

We saw the show at the New Yorker featuring beautiful Mary Over, who I had seen in Ice Vogues of 1947 in Tampa. My father took me to Peck & Goodie (the salesman there said that Arnold Shoda had been playing cards, upstairs, earlier) for my first pair of ice figure skates (Riedell boots and Olympiad "North American" blades), and then up to Iceland above the lobby of Madison Square Garden for the beginning of my transition to ice!

I could do loop jumps and split jumps my second time out, but skating forward was tough, as I kept going over the toe picks, leaning too far forward. There were three or so skaters from the Center Theater practicing behind a rope on the end patch, so I went back there with them, to flail around with split jumps, interspersed, which they seemed to think was funny. I heard one of the boy skaters say to the girl that she needed to spend more time at practice and less on "other activities"... kinda' an eye opener for teenage me!

We went on to Atlantic City, where I saw Ice Capades for the first time, starring Donna Atwood, Bobby Specht, and the gang -- Jimmy Lawrence and Margaret Field were also doing the star roles at some performances, but the show I watched was with Atwood and Specht. Returning home to Florida, after a little skate at Jones Beach, I had one more school year in which to cool my heels before going to the University of Pennsylvania and the Philadelphia Skating Club & Humane Society for a permanent marriage with the ice.

Video links of me at Jones Beach and Arnold Shoda at the Chicago Hilton:
https://www.youtube.com/watch?v=nwOuBmfjclw
https://www.youtube.com/watch?v=YCK4dGGy550

The author, Carl Moseley, at Jones Beach

The author's Dad, Carl H. Moseley, toweling off at the beach in Atlantic City

Carl observing the Jefferson Memorial in Washington, D.C.

Chapter Sixty-One
Barrels & Stilts & Penguins

After seeing *Holiday On Ice* for the first time in 1947 in Tampa, when my dad was the Promoter, I saw it every year, and haunted backstage until I went north to college in 1952, and finally got on the ice!

I remember walking on the Bayshore in Tampa after roller skating practice, dreaming about traveling with *Holiday On Ice*! For six years in Philadelphia I saw only Ice Capades and Ice Follies, but haunted them, too, at the Arena in Philadelphia, and worked on my skating continually at the Philadelphia Skating Club & H.S. and at the Arena.

In fact, I auditioned for Ice Follies in 1958. Fran Claudet told me I was too tall to match up in the Swing Waltz.

Returning to Tampa, I again saw *Holiday On Ice* of 1959, and by then Tommy Allen Weinreich and Janie Morris were in the show. Jack Jost, another pro at the PSC&HS, had told me about Tommy's joining the show, suggesting that I, too, think of auditioning for HOI, but I got into the rink business, instead. The summer before Janie joined the show, I met her at Bill Barg and Mary Bohland's rink at Lakewood Fairgrounds in Atlanta (where Fran Pappas was teaching), and did some lifts with gorgeous "Miss Georgia" Janie Morris, even before she did them with Alfredo Mendoza -- one with a hilarious ending!

"My Story" by Carl Moseley

When the first major ice show in Florida, Ice Vogues of 1947, played my dad's building, the Coliseum in Tampa, we had a boxy Kodak 16 mm movie camera with which we wanted to get some footage of the show. The available film, those days, was not fast enough to film inside with the show lighting, so my dad and I asked some of the skaters to step out back in costume, before going on, for a pose or two.

Barrel jumper/stilt skater Georg Von Birgelen accommodated us, but got very nervous, as it was a windy day, in fear that the paper hoop he was carrying might be ripped, before he got a chance to jump through it! Unfortunately, when I got this old 16 mm film out to copy to DVD, I found that it had all crumbled with age.

My father, Carl H. Moseley, got a bit upset that first year that Ice Vogues producer and star skater, Everett McGowan, who also owned and maintained the portable rink tank, suffered a slight injury in doing some maintenance with a compressor, and feared it might keep Everett, of McGowan & Mack, out of the show. It did not, thankfully.

Georg Von Birgelen

McGowan & Mack

Annie Schmidt (right) as a penguin in a number featuring Loismarie Goeller (Van Ormer) in Holiday On Ice of 1948 (U.S.A.) (full photo below)

"My Story" by Carl Moseley

For *Holiday On Ice* of 1948 (U.S.A.) I had the run of the building, the Armory, since my dad was the promoter in Tampa. The stage manager once told me to go call "five" for kicks, and followed me about backstage, saying LOUDER!

There was a number featuring penguins, with Annie Schmidt, Loismarie Goeller (Van Ormer), and others. I was sitting behind the set one show when the penguin gals came out of their dressing room, all decked out, with cardboard white penguin chests, and a chorus boy went up to one cute gal (maybe his girlfriend), and started rapping out a little rhythm on her hard, white chest... I didn't quite know what to make of that.

Annie was quite versatile, later becoming performance director and assistant to choreographer Chester Hale.

Georg Von Birgelen

(Below) Holiday On Ice refrigeration unit in earlier times, on the trailer, showing compressor, condenser (somewhere), and huge brine chiller tank with 4" hose leading to the 4" Header pipes on each side of the rink floor.

Right: A model of the very first ice making machine, and below a photo of Dr. John Gorrie, inventor of same.

Gorrie School, Tampa, Florida, named for Dr. John Gorrie -- This is where the author went to elementary school!

"My Story" by Carl Moseley

Elvis loved visiting *Holiday On Ice* while in the Army in Europe, and he kept up his friendship with the show back in the States. He invited the cast to Graceland in Memphis for a party or two, and he would rent the local amusement park after hours and have all the kids from the show join him on the rides.

Elvis and friends!

Elvis with Guy Longpre

Chapter Sixty-Two

Looking Back

Before *Holiday On Ice* and my rink in Florida, I had six skating years in Philadelphia at the Philadelphia Skating Club & Humane Society and the Philadelphia Arena. My best two years there were in 1957 and 1958 after graduating from the University of Pennsylvania (and a six-month active tour with the U.S. Army, squeezed in-between).

I took the six-day-a-week job at the Philadelphia Skating Club running all the Jr. Club Sessions, including teaching some classes and a few privates, which also allowed me lots of ice time. I would arrive at the Club early mornings and patch often, then free skate the morning Sr. Club session, with pro Melitta Brunner as a skating "pal" and weekly lessons with Hans Johnsen, who had become a good friend, too!

Joan Ferguson, whose dad was first chair violist in the Philadelphia Orchestra, once took me to a concert and up backstage at intermission, where stood casually Eugene Ormandy! She was a good skating buddy, and we messed around with a few pair moves, once knocking down Hans Johnsen, who was giving an dance lesson!

"My Story" by Carl Moseley

After the morning skate, I might shower in the locker room (sometimes shave, too), and then catch a quick lunch at the snack bar before going out again on an hour or so of dead ice time to work on some figures and free skate a bit, too, to my own music which I could put on in the sound control cubicle.

Then it was time to run the afternoon Jr. Club Sessions -- 1,000 kids divided into four age groups, with two sessions for each, weekly. Lucy Lee Flippin, who later skated in *Holiday On Ice*, was in the high school group. After, these sessions, I went back out for all-out free skating practice- on the 5:00 to 6:00 Competitors' Hour, on which Ray Balmer (Raymond Bloomer) was our top skater, and others.

Leaving the rink, I headed for my second job as a waiter at the family Italian restaurant, the Roma, back in West Philadelphia near the Arena and the U. of P., where I got a free meal, tips, and $1.00/day, but the food was worth it -- all the food I wanted, and quarts of daily homemade soups, plus Italian bread to take home for my wife, then, Linda Moseley, along with an entree for her.

While at the Roma restaurant, I waited on Grace Kelly's brother-in-law (whose daughter, Meg Davis, was a top Philadelphia skater) and his family, and on Sundays in came chorus gals from Ice Follies and Ice Capades, between shows!

At the PSC&HS, we had many special events such a Judges' Schools, which I attended, and tons of top skaters & coaches came in to give exhibitions and lectures, including Ron Ludington (whom I had met before at roller Nationals), Lynn Patsy Finnegan, Alain Calmat and Alain Giletti, Don Jacoby, Carol Heiss, pros Pierre Brunet and Gus Lussi, among others -- lots to soak up, in those days!

See color photo section:
The Philadelphia Skating Club &
Humane Society
and
A plate of spaghetti and meatballs

"My Story" by Carl Moseley

Chapter Sixty-Three
Corralling the Jr. Club Kids

A few more reflections, looking back on my time at the Philadelphia Skating Club & H.S. before *Holiday On Ice*... I ran all of the Jr. Club sessions, including things like relay races, which they were crazy about (to blow off steam), and otherwise kept the sessions orderly and organized with various activities that promoted skating learning and kept down "cracking the whip" or dangerously chasing each other around if things got boring!

All four pros, including me, each taught a class or two in the older groups, and I taught all the "tots." I demonstrated a simple routine (mimeographed on two or three sheets, and created by one of the Jr. Club board ladies) for the youngest kids to perform in the Jr. Club competition. The older kids could be a handful, and Lucy Lee Flippin and her buddy Brenda Fritche (who did a similar pair), liked to give me a hard time, in a friendly way. They did keep me busy!

Ed Flinterman, the PSC&HS Manager and also a Wharton graduate from my school, the University of Pennsylvania, allowed me to teach privates in the hugely crowded (800 or so, often) Friday night public sessions, and ultimately rope off a patch at the end, to do so. A source of great satisfaction to me were the three Jr. Club members I coached to the Philadelphia Area Championships in 1958. All three medaled, including a Juvenile Boy, and the two little gals, Susan Bromer and Lesanne Walters, I coached in Similar Pairs, who Silvered against the great Batdorf twins, Ann and Mary, from Hershey!

To show how small the skating world can be, Dorian Shields Valles was 1970 U.S. National Novice Ladies Champion with her coach Evy Scotvold, who married Mary, one of the Batdorf twins!

I had to take Susan and Lesanne to the rink at Valley Forge occasionally, to get enough ice time to choreograph their numbers. I also taught Lesanne free style with my friend and pro Hans Johnsen. Lesanne medaled in Singles, too, at the Philadelphia Areas, due to our joint effort.

The closing move in Susan and Lesanne's Pair was a "Catch Pair Flying Camel," which I now see in videos that Randy Gardner and Tai Babilonia did as a closing move in an Ice Capades number. Susan Bromer and Lesanne Walters went on to be USFSA Gold Figure Medalists in later years. A high point, too, in those days was when I drove Melitta Brunner (I used to drive her all over the "main line" as Melitta, herself, didn't drive) to Hans Johnsen's home for dinner, and Hans invited me to join them, toasting at the table: "Well, now that we have the three greatest minds in skating all together, we can solve all the problems that may arise!" Spoken in jest, of course, but still a kick!

As mentioned before, Melitta skated many morning sessions at the PSC&HS with me. Mellita was an inspiration and did a very nice loop jump, in her own style. I tried to get her to work on axels, but she said: "I'll leave the axels to you!"

See color photo section:
Dorian Shields Valles
and later Holiday On Ice skater,
Lucy Lee Flippin

"My Story" by Carl Moseley

Hans Johnsen

Chapter Sixty-Four
Inspiration In Philly

Many show and pro skaters came in to the Spring and Fall open sessions at the Philadelphia Skating Club & HS and also skated at the Philadelphia Arena. My skating buddy, Joan Ferguson, pointed out a very pretty and elegant gal skater one day, saying her name was Gerry Mahoney of Ice Capades, and indeed it was Gerry Tilghman (Mahoney), Mother of skater & Facebook friend Bill Tilghman!

Billy Kipp, who was on the fated 1961 plane to Worlds, came from Allentown in his days before coaching Peggy Fleming and was an inspiration to watch with his smooth and innovative steps, and gave me a few tips, too!

Danny Ryan, also on that 1961 flight, and also a singles competitor on rollers, was lots of fun on the ice as we tried different moves. I hacked around with Doug Searfoss, Doug Sears, later, in Ice Follies, Pairs Champion at South and I think Mid-Atlantics. Doug and I had a little contest one afternoon at the PSC&HS to see who could do the most Axels in a row without a step in between -- I did ten; Doug did twelve!

"My Story" by Carl Moseley

Barbara Myers, also a former roller skater, showed up one day and was very interesting to talk with and lovely to watch on the ice. At the Philadelphia Arena, and the Sunday morning club sessions of the International Skating Club of Philadelphia, appeared Marie McClenahan, former Eastern Sr. Ladies Champion and Ice Cycles principal, as well as a star with Arnold Shoda at the New York Roxy Theater. Later, as Marie Pearce, she became a top USFSA official and World Judge!

Bob Scrak, with Ice Capades, invited me onto Ice Capades practice ice at the Philadelphia Arena, but I was told by another Ice Capades skater that I might lose my USFSA amateur status for being on it with pros, so I got off fast!

Holiday On Ice of 1948 skater Charlie Ward, working on his PhD in Physics at Penn, lived across the street from me in another brownstone, and advised me on liquor (no!), and women (yes, but with advice and consolation, which I sorely needed at the time). Charlie married a nurse, two flights up, soon after. I took Charlie, just a great guy, to the PSC&HS one day as a guest to put his skates on again, and when the Hollywood Ice Revue came to Philadelphia, Charlie Ward took me along to visit with Bobby Blake and Jack Rose.

George Manuel, from Ice Follies, was able to do his clockwise double axels against the traffic, somehow, in a public session at the PSC&HS, and he encouraged me on my jumps, as well. Of course, I would see often at the Club Don Jacoby, U.S. Dance Champion and later Ice Follies star, and Don, as a senior at the U. of Penn., coached me in a solo stage dance number in the freshman "Mask & Wig" show -- russian splits, double air turns, and all!

On entering the PSC&HS rink in Ardmore, once, I saw Joe Marshall in the midst of a flying camel on the ice, and I got my skates on quickly to meet and join Joe for some unusually empty great ice time! Kathy Kay Brabson was a young skater then, in Philadelphia, before Kathy Kay joined Ice Follies, for a fine career. I know there are a couple more of these great inspirational "gypsies" that I might have missed... please forgive any omissions.

Video of Barbara Myers:
https://www.youtube.com/watch?v=zLgfJYLR-Vk

Gerry Mahoney (Tilghman) & Hollywood friends

Danny Ryan & partner

See color photo section:
Ice Follies program page featuring Barbara Myers

"My Story" by Carl Moseley

Ice Follies program page featuring Doug Sears

Chapter Sixty-Five
A Tale of Rome

During my last two years at the Philadelphia Skating Club & H.S., running the Jr. Club sessions and teaching in order to make ends meet, I had a second job as a waiter at a neighborhood Italian restaurant in West Philadelphia near our apartment and the Philadelphia Arena. The owner, Corrado (Carl in English) Costa, and his brother had once operated a chain of restaurants in Philadelphia, but Corrado was now down to this one homey family spot. "Family" it was, with Corrado: Joe, the Italian chef; old Nick, a Greek career waiter; David, a dental student waiter; and me. Corrado's nephew would come in on our busy Sundays as salad chef, to make salads and cut desserts, but otherwise we three waiters would do both, as well as all busing, taking orders, and serving.

Two fellows were dishwashers in the kitchen, but once when they didn't show up David and I became the dishwashers, too. I knew nothing about waiting tables to start with, but David coached me, sometimes in an impatient, chastising way, but I caught on quickly, and learned to keep the silverware racks full, grind the fresh Romano cheese from the block, and carry two, and sometimes three, dinner plates (we had no trays) at once.

"My Story" by Carl Moseley

I would arrive there in time for the late dinner hour on week-days, after catching the 5:00-6:00 p.m. "Competitors Hour" free skate at the PSC&HS, and worked 5:00-8:00 p.m. Saturdays and all day Sunday, when we were slammed from noon to 8:00 p.m.! I was so busy, meeting myself going in and out of the kitchen, on Sundays, that I was too tired and had almost no appetite for my free meal at Sundays end!

We would try to help each other, and Corrado would step in and take orders and pick up a waiting plate or two from the kitchen. Old Nick, when in a bind, would say to me, in passing: "Gotta' help me - Gotta' help me," and I would, the best I could!

We received $1.00 a day, tips, and a full course dinner, consisting of soup or salad, entree, dessert, and a beverage. Often, I would make myself a big Italian salad, and on weekday evenings munch on that, going back and forth, and if there was an untouched meatball on a plate, covered with tomato sauce, it never made it back to the kitchen -- I would pop in into my mouth with a fork, on the way!

In this manner, I could take home my plate entree for my wife, then, Linda (whom I would pick up from her job when I left the Roma) for her dinner, plus a quart of daily home-made soup -- lentil, tomato rice, split pea, or minestrone-vegetable. Corrado was happy for me to have it, as Joe made fresh soup each day, and they only threw the leftovers away. Add some Italian bread, and we were good to go.

I soon found out, however, that we waiters were limited to the less exotic meals on the menu, as when I gave my order to Joe for veal scallopine parmiagana, he said: "E' no for you!" after which David explained that this and chicken cacciatore were not on our plates! Not to worry however, as the spaghetti and meatballs, my favorite, was the best I ever had, anywhere, and plain breaded Veal cutlet was delicious.

For his own dinners, Joe, the chef, would have just a plate of plain pasta spaghetti, maybe "alli-ollie," garlic and oil, while sitting at a low stool and counter, back in the kitchen. The "kitchen" was a converted garage, with a rough concrete floor and three or four cats that wandered in nightly, to whom Joe would throw scraps of meat, which, of course, the cats gobbled up voraciously. I'll never forget how Joe, to make sure food on the plates stayed hot, would spin two large dinner plates, one in each bare hand in boiling water, before dishing up an entree on each! Joe would also squeeze off, bare-handed, portions of al-dente spaghetti from the boiling pot, too!

As the Roma was just a stone's throw from the Philadelphia Arena, Ice Capades and Ice Follies gals would sometime come in on Sundays between shows, and I would enjoy serving them. Musicians would often come in too, bringing their own wine, as we did not serve any alcohol.

I once served the large family of Grace Kelly's brother-in-law who owned the local hockey team, was president of the the International Skating Club of Philadelphia, and whose daughter, Meg Davis, was the top amateur Philadelphia skater of the day. Two people who were known non-tippers were avoided, if possible, particularly the one who always wanted his coffee cup filled more, to the brim, or wanted it sent back and re-filled, as not hot enough!

There were two sisters, dinner regulars who operated the beauty parlor next door, who tipped conservatively, but were always congenial. The biggest conundrum was a table of four football players from my school, Penn, who consumed the Italian bread like water. After the third helping, owner Corrado would say to me: "You charge them, you charge them!" for the extra bread. Of course that's all I needed to do to kiss my tip bye-bye after walking my butt off for these base-price spaghetti eating goons!

One memorable day Corrado's widowed sister-in-law, still part owner, I guess, waltzed in, very unhappy about how operations were going, and began screaming and throwing plates about the kitchen. The large, heavy dinner plates would hit that rough concrete floor and loudly split, spinning in all directions. Corrado yelled to me: "Call the wagon-call the wagon!" (the police), which I proceeded to attempt to do on our one pay phone in the corner of the dining room. The result of all this was the closing of the Roma restaurant for a few weeks (during which all the food in the walk-in coolers spoiled from no electric service), until a court order was issued placing Corrado Costa in full charge, and off limits to his dangerous sister-in-law. With the Roma once again in operation, I was back to enjoy the best spaghetti & meatballs the world has ever known!

"My Story" by Carl Moseley

Pictured below is the fireplace in our Delta Tau Delta fraternity house, at the University of Pennsylvania in Philadelphia. Behind the fireplace common wall was the Delta Upsulon house. As a Delt pledge were were required during "hell week" to get down on our knees facing the fireplace and moosehead, and bend up and down, arms raised, and recite: "All praises be to the Delta Moose, whose ass end is in the DU hoose!"

One activity during "hell week" involved all 15 of us "pledges" starting on the third floor, in athletic shorts, taking a mouthful of a concoction from a large tub (water, vinegar, pepper, ketchup, and something else) and crawling down on our hands and knees to spit into the fireplace, and yell out: "I'm putting out the Delt fire!" and then crawl back up the stairs to the third floor for another mouthful!

On the day we finally became "brothers," in a ceremony in front of this fireplace, we were all toasted with brandy by all our upperclass Delta Tau Delta brothers, and each of us passed by the fireplace and hurled our glasses into it as a ritual of passage... *Another time, another place...*

The Delta Tay Delta fireplace and moosehead

Chapter Sixty-Six

Escape & Evasion

Between my working and teaching years at the Philadelphia Skating Club & H.S. in 1957 and 1958, I went on active duty for six months with the U.S. Army, as a 2nd Lt. for Officer's Basic Training. I had already had my six weeks of R.O.T.C. "boot" camp two summers before. I started at the Infantry School in Fort Benning, Georgia, and then for two more months as a staff officer for an enlisted basic training company at Fort Jackson, South Carolina.

While at Fort Benning, one third of our training was at night, with helicopter landings in pitch black areas, armored personnel carriers barely floating, crossing the Chatahoochee River, etc., to emulate realistic combat situations as much as possible. One "night problem" called "Escape And Evasion" sticks in my memory.

Fort Benning goes on for miles and miles of vine-tangled backwoods and rough terrain, ravines bordering creeks, etc. south of the main military post. We were taken out in 2 1/2 ton trucks (our primary means of transportation during training problems) to a remote

"My Story" by Carl Moseley

Georgia clay road, "Red Diamond Road" was one. We were dropped off, one by one, about 100 yards apart at sunset, and our mission was to get back to "friendly lines" eight miles away across this unknown wilderness -- snakes, creeks, vines, and all, without being captured by "agressor troops" by sunup the next day.

We were supposed to stay separated from our buddies, but as the night went on, after stumbling down to a creek bed or two (at least one broken leg resulted, but not in our Company), and cutting through tangled vines, we ended up in groups of three or four to cut open some cans of "C" rations and try to get some shut-eye in tank trails, for warmth. Even in Georgia, it was cool in the dead of night.

I had managed to avoid the "aggressor troops", seeing flashes of blank gunfire though the trees, and hearing shouts, as some of our guys were captured and and hauled off to "prison" compounds for "interrogation" (minus one boot so they could not jump off the 3/4 ton trucks hauling them away).

Just as it was becoming light, a couple of "aggressors" spotted me, however, and I hauled butt as fast as I could to get away. I never ran as fast in my life! I finally jumped down a slope and under a clump of bushes, where I choked to keep my exhausted breathing quiet as they nosed around close by looking for me! Finally they gave up, and wandered off, looking for more officer trainees to capture, so I came out of hiding and found my way back to "friendly lines" at dawn... and freedom... to return later to the PSC&HS!

"My Story" by Carl Moseley

Carl and Linda Moseley performing a spread eagle

Carl Moseley in flight!

ABOUT THE AUTHOR...

CARL L. MOSELEY saw his first ice show, Ice Vogues of 1947, at his dad's building in Tampa, Florida. Only 13 years old at the time, he was "blown away and hooked!" He began competing on roller skates (as there was no ice in Florida), and won Gold in Pairs and Fours at the Southern U.S. Championships in 1950.

In 1952, Carl attended the University of Pennsylvania and made the switch to ice, skating at the historic Philadephia Skating Club & Humane Society. Four years later, he became a Jr. Pro at the Club.

He spent four years touring with *Holiday On Ice* from 1965 to 1968, as Assistant Company Manager to Tommy Collins. Over the years he also performed several other jobs in the company, including skating in the show. He also filmed many of the show numbers using his 8 mm movie camera, thereby preserving quite a bit of show skating history.

Many of his films of those early years were published by the Pro Skating Historical Foundation as *The Golden Age of Ice Shows*.

Carl was a Captain in the U.S. Army, graduating from the Infantry School at Fort Benning, Georgia. He earned a B.S. in Economics from the Wharton School of the University of Pennsylvania.

After his years touring with the ice shows, he became a US Figure Skating Association judge, a skating coach, and a rink owner. Together, Carl and his wife at the time, Linda, were majority stockholders in a rink corporation that leased and operated Iceland in St. Petersburg for nine years, sending many skaters to Holiday On Ice and Ice Capades, too! He also managed movie theater and other entertainment businesses.

A frequent poster on the Facebook page for the Pro Skating Historical Foundation, Carl delights many readers with photos and comments about the world of ice show skating.

In this book, he wanted to pass on his memories of those four years -- to share his enjoyment of the thrilling performances and fascinating stars, as well as his knowledge of the ice show business from "behind the scenes."